William Dreghorn 1908 - 2001

William Dreghhorn was a remarkable educator, author and illustrator, but above all he will be remembered as an enthusiastic teacher of geology who used clear descriptions and field sketches to explain the most complex landscapes. While teaching at St. Paul's College, Cheltenham, now the University of Gloucestershire, he published Geology Explained in the Severn Vale and Cotswolds, and Geology Explained in the Forest of Dean and Wye Valley. He then moved to Northern Cyprus, where he became a well-known authority on landscape and archaeology. His later books included Landscapes in North Cyprus, Beaches of the North Cyprus Coast, Rocks and Scenery in the Kyrenia Region, Guide to the Antiquities of Kyrenia and Antiquities of Nicosia.

Geology Explained in the Forest of Dean and Wye Valley

by
William Dreghorn BSc FRGS

Illustrated by the Author

Fineleaf Editions

Copyright © William Dreghorn, David & Charles, 1968

Acknowledgments
The author wishes to record his thanks to Mr R Bradshaw MSc, lecturer in the Department of Geology, University of Bristol, for his scientific advice and guidance, to Mrs L Durrant BA of Lydney, for her patience in correcting the script and to John Head BSc, for kindly helping with the proofs. He would also like to express his appreciation of help given by members of the Forest of Dean Caving Society and other residents in the area, particularly Mr Raymond Wright of Cinderford and Mr Richard Morgan of Ruardean for their valuable help in giving information about iron and coal mining. The author, however, is responsible for all the opinions expressed in the book. To a serious geologist the treatment in this book may seem somewhat superficial, but the author's aim is to popularise geology and this book is intended as an introduction to the geology of an area much used by students. WD 1968

Rock exposures and geological maps
Many of the quarries and cliffs described by the author have deteriorated considerably since he wrote this book: a number are now on private land, with no right of access, and some are in dangerous condition. British Geological Survey maps at 1:50,000 scale cover most of the area. These are available from BGS at Keyworth, Nottingham NG12 5GG. Telephone 0115 936 3241 or email: sales@bgs.ac.uk

Design: Philip Gray
Typeset in Adobe Garamond Pro
Print: Print Solutions Partnership

First published by David and Charles, 1968
Published by Fineleaf Editions 2005
www.fineleaf.co.uk
Studio Two, Parkfields, Pontshill, Ross-on-Wye HR9 5TH

ISBN: 978-0-9534437-1-0

British Library Cataloguing in Publication Data
A catalogue record for this book is available from the British Library

Except as otherwise permitted under the Copyright, Designs and Patents Act, 1988, this publication may only be reproduced, stored or transmitted in any form or by any means, with the prior permission of the publisher, or, in the case of reprographic reproduction, in accordance with the terms of a licence issued by The Copyright Licensing Agency.

Index

Introduction to the First Edition		7
Chapter 1	The Geology of the Region	9
Chapter 2	The Rocks and how they were Formed	14
Chapter 3	The Main Structures of the Region	19
Chapter 4	A Traverse of the Dean Syncline	27
Chapter 5	The Littledean and Ruspidge Areas	36
Chapter 6	The Blakeney-Soudley Area	43
Chapter 7	Lydney Area & Beachley-Clanna Pericline	50
Chapter 8	Hope Mansel Dome & Wigpool Syncline	59
Chapter 9	The Wye Valley: Ross to Kerne Bridge	67
Chapter 10	The Symond's Yat Area	76
Chapter 11	Wye Valley: Monmouth Area	92
Chapter 12	Wye Valley: Monmouth to Tintern Abbey	98
Chapter 13	Wye Valley: Tintern to Chepstow	111
Chapter 14	The Scowles	124
Chapter 15	The Origin of the Iron Ore	136
Chapter 16	The Coal Measures: Scenery and Mining	141
Chapter 17	The Origin of Coal in the Forest of Dean	152
Chapter 18	Some Geological Curiosities	158
Glossary of Terms		169
Bibliography		173
Appendix: Table of rock strata		175
Index		177

Introduction to the First Edition

THE AIM OF THIS BOOK is to explain geology in terms of scenery in an area which is visited every year by thousands of tourists who for the most part are well educated but were never introduced to the subject of geology in their school days. It is hoped that it will be the means of developing in these visitors to the Forest of Dean and Wye Valley an eye for scenery in the sense that it is to a large extent controlled and formed by the underlying strata of rocks. The miners of iron and coal in this region had a particularly keen appreciation of variations in the scenery for they could tell from these where outcrops of coal and iron were likely to be. This knowledge could effect their livelihood but, for the tourist, the study will be a form of mental recreation with an educational slant.

The Forest of Dean is the region between the rivers Severn and Wye. Its name originated in the twelfth century and we should include the Wye valley as a sub-region of the forest itself. Since the opening of the Severn bridge in 1966, there have been many more visitors to these two regions and possible new towns in the Severn Vale could further increase their numbers. It is to be hoped that the Forestry Commission, which has done excellent work in developing the Forest and in providing camping grounds, 'nature trails' and rambling routes for true nature lovers, will be able to co-operate with the planners to preserve these areas as a social amenity for future generations.

Geology is essentially a field science and the writer spent at least three days every week for a couple of years rambling over the area with the usual geologist's equipment, including the six inches to the mile geological map. Readers of this book will not require such a map but they would do well to purchase the one inch to the mile geological maps, the Chepstow and Monmouth sheets. The writer walked over the region thinking with the map, tapping the rocks in the various quarries and making his own interpretations in addition to reading the literature published by various geologists who have studied this area during the past century. 'A picture is worth a thousand words' says the Chinese proverb, and as geological maps are rather difficult to understand the text is illustrated with many block diagrams. These are made by selecting a good viewpoint, carefully drawing the scene and then, so to speak, cutting through it to reveal the underlying strata. In this way the control exercised by layers of rock (strata) can be related to the physical features of the landscape. Here it must be noted that in the block diagram the dip or slope of the strata is not true because of the exaggeration of the vertical height of the hills in proportion to the length of the diagram. In most cases the actual dip of the strata will be shown in an appended note.

In the field, one can learn a good deal by sketching the landscape, for not only is this a very satisfying and relaxing hobby but it forces the amateur artist really to study the hills, rocks, crags and valleys he is drawing. He is obliged to consider scenic features and the reasons for the shapes of the hills. Another pleasant way of learning geology is to adjourn to an inn at the end of a day's tramp and talk to local miners, some of whom may have worked for twenty years in coal mines or delved into the limestones seeking pockets of iron ore. These are the practical geologists from whom one can learn a tremendous amount.

Finally a word of warning about entering quarries in the region to be explored. Many are mentioned throughout this book and in all cases permission to enter must first be sought. Even though they may be wired up and obviously closed, owners often use such places for storage and sometimes, bee-keeping.

Chapter 1
The Geology of the Region

'WHAT is the point of geology?' is the obvious opening question to this chapter, and a short answer could be that geologists are employed in searching in the rocks for the raw materials required for industry, eg North Sea gas, oil, coal, metals, clays for bricks and pottery, limestone for cement and the natural materials used for nuclear power. As only small numbers of professional geologists are required, the scope for employment is rather limited and this is one of the reasons why geology is seldom taught as a school subject. It is significant, however, that it is taught in many Welsh schools and this may be partly due to the Welsh avidity for culture and partly because the rocks loom up behind the schools, ever reminding the Principality that its chief exports are coal and school teachers!

Geology is really the history of the Earth or part of 'Earth Science' as it is termed in the United States. The best way to start on this subject is to study the local geology and this point is stressed in a recent memorandum published by the Geological Society as part of an enquiry by the British Association for the Advancement of Science into the teaching of geology in schools. The memorandum declares that teachers of geology should first become experts in local geology–and what finer place could such a teacher have than the Forest of Dean and Wye Valley, where the rocks on the doorstep can be studied in pleasant surroundings. Gloucestershire is very fortunate geologically for almost every known rock formation in Britain can be found within the county. How this came about is explained by Figures 1A and 1B.

It will be seen from Figure 1A that the rocks on the western side of the Severn are labelled Palaeozoic, meaning 'ancient life', while those on the eastern side are termed Mesozoic, meaning 'middle life'. It was William Smith (1769-1839) who first declared that rocks could be identified by the assemblage of fossils within them, and Palaeozoic rocks contain much more ancient forms of life than the Mesozoic. The former period began about 600 million years ago and ended 225 million years before the present. These rocks tend to be harder and usually form higher ground, often with a rugged relief. Mesozoic rocks are not only younger but in general softer, thus forming a more subdued relief, though there are exceptions in the highest point of the Cotswolds at Cleeve Hill, 1,070 feet and the Forest of Dean at 951 feet. Mesozoic rocks are not found

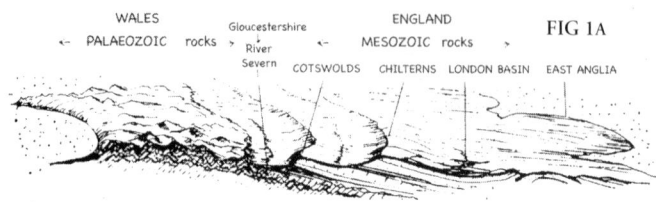

A diagram map to show how older rocks are in Wales and most of the younger rocks are in England. It also explains why Gloucestershire has a variety of rocks from Wales and England.

in the Forest of Dean and this factor sharpens the contrast in scenery between the Welsh borderlands and the Cotswolds.

Before going further, it is most important to understand the real meaning of geological time, and many experts in the subject fail to realise how difficult it is for the human mind to comprehend such terms as 'hundreds of millions of years'. Let us first get a notion of a million. If a thousand books, each two inches wide, were placed on a shelf they would stretch for fifty yards, while a million such books would continue for thirty miles. Geologists tell us that the Earth is about 4,500 million years old, a very difficult time factor to grasp. A million DAYS ago takes us back to 772 BC, a time when Iron Age tribes occupied such settlements as the one at Symond's Yat (the earthworks were subsequently used as Offa's Dyke in the eighth century AD). About ten million DAYS ago Palaeolithic men were living in King Arthur's Cave, near Symond's Yat, and sallying forth each day to hunt wild animals. A million YEARS ago a type related to Man inhabited some parts of the world. This was the age of Man-apes. To a geologist, all this is very recent time for he has to deal with rocks whose age is measured in hundreds of millions of years. Geological time, or Geochronometry, can be ascertained in a relative way by examining fossils in rocks, but if none is present the age of a certain stratum must be deduced from the surrounding rocks. More recently, the method of isotopic age dating has been developed. Rocks are aggregates of minerals and in some, very minute traces of radioactive elements are found. On the assumption that radioactive decay proceeds at a constant rate for a particular isotope, the age of rocks can be determined by measuring the amount of decayed material. This provides a very handy geological clock with which to estimate the ages of rocks, independent of the relative dates given by fossils.

The Geology of the Region

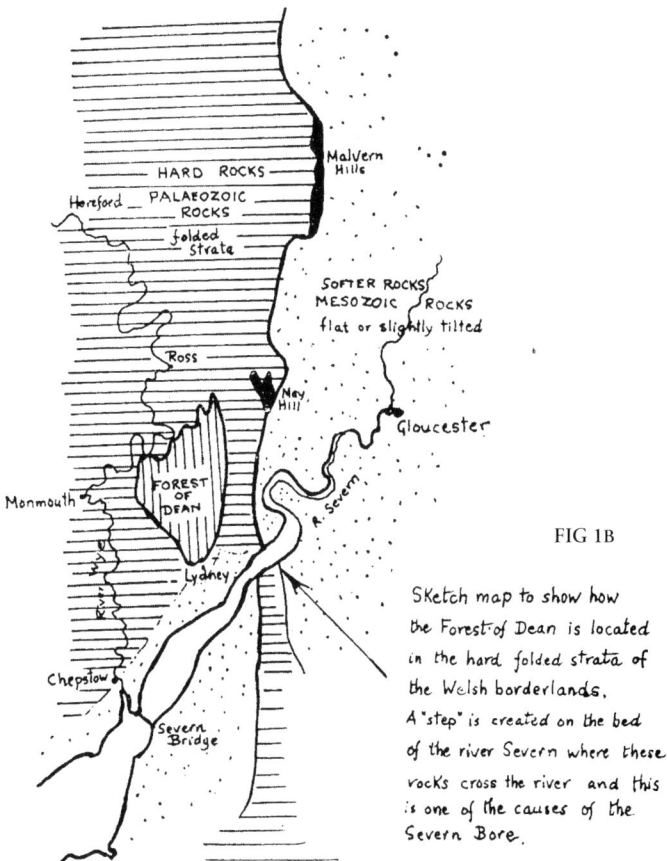

FIG 1B

Sketch map to show how the Forest of Dean is located in the hard folded strata of the Welsh borderlands. A "step" is created on the bed of the river Severn where these rocks cross the river and this is one of the causes of the Severn Bore.

Usually there is close agreement, whichever method is used.

At the beginning of the Palaeozoic era some 600 million years ago, Britain was part of a land mass linking Canada to Europe. It was like a pavement of crystalline rocks in which cracks ran in parallel groups revealing weaknesses in the Earth's crust. Although in the last 600 million years, great thicknesses of sediment have been laid down on the pavement, these structural lines of weakness have re-asserted

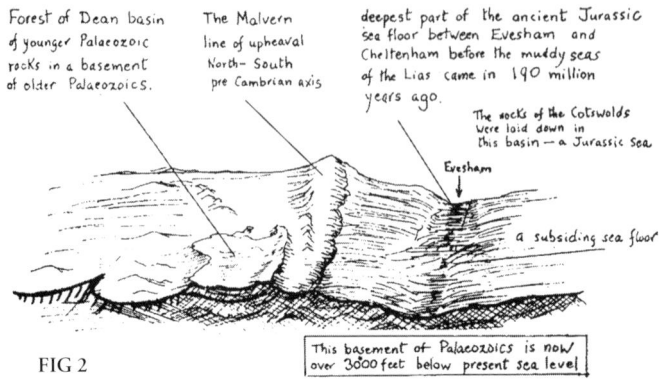

FIG 2

The scene during the Triassic deserts some 200 million years ago. The Forest of Dean was already in the making as a distinct area. It remained a land mass when the seas of Jurassic times (Mesozoic) invaded the axial depression stretching from the Midlands to the Mendips.

themselves from time to time in the form of great faults or in folds along their axial lines. Hence the geological dictum, 'Once a line of weakness, always a line of weakness'—implying that folds often occur in the same places. A good example of this is the Malvern Line which runs in a north-south direction, and similar lines can be traced in other parts of Britain. It is this Malvern Axial Line which has not only controlled the folding of the strata in the Forest of Dean but has frequently caused the sediments to be different on either side in both the Palaeozoic and Mesozoic eras.

At the beginning of the Mesozoic era there was a saucer-shaped depression filled with younger Palaeozoic rocks within a basement of older rocks lying to the south-east of the great land mass of which Wales was just a part. The diagram, Figure 2, shows the probable type of country some 225 million years ago, when the great Permian and Triassic deserts stretched from the Mendips to Cheshire. It can be seen from the diagram that the Forest of Dean region was already a structural unit over 200 million years ago. The Mesozoic era was ushered in by the Trias and later came the invasion of the Jurassic seas into a sinking land area that lay between Yorkshire and Devon. The deepest part of this subsiding sea floor lay between Cheltenham and Evesham, where great thicknesses of Lias clays were deposited. The region of Wales and its borderlands west of the Malvern Axis was probably dry land at this time, and the rocks in our region were subjected to continued erosion which revealed more and more of the underlying structures. The Palaeozoic rocks of Wales and the Forest of Dean continue as a basement right across the country to the London Basin. A remarkable map, published by the Geological Survey in 1966 and using information obtained from boreholes and seismic surveys, shows the actual depths of this basement below present ground level. In places, this ancient floor is more than 3,000 feet below present sea level. On a scale of 25 inches to the mile this 'Tectonic Map of Great Britain and Northern Ireland' provides much information about the origin of the rocks in Gloucestershire.

Chapter 2

The Rocks and how they were Formed

FOR the nature lover, perhaps it is only necessary at first to identify rocks by their colours as revealed in quarries, crags, cliffs, roadside and railway cuttings. Later, but with much practice in the field, he should be able to recognise many rocks by the minerals they contain. This is the division of geology known as 'petrology'. Proceeding further, he should be able to designate a stratum by the fossils in it. The student of palaeontology, as this is called, will need that excellent book, British Palaeozoic Fossils Published by the Natural History Museum. On the basis of colour, the following rocks can be easily seen in the Forest of Dean and Wye valley:

1. The red rocks which are mainly sandstones belonging to the Devonian system, the usual term being Old Red Sandstone.
2. White to pinkish grey limestones of the Carboniferous Limestone series.
3. Pink to yellow sandstones, the Drybrook Sandstone also of the Carboniferous Limestone series.
4. Grey sandstones of the Pennant series. Upper Coal Measures (mainly found in the core of the Forest).

The table on page at the end of this book gives the list of strata to be found in this area with the oldest rocks at the bottom and the youngest at the top, a logical sequence for this is how they would be found if, after being deposited, they had never been disturbed by earth movements. Although average thicknesses of rocks are given, it must be remembered that strata will vary considerably in thickness from place to place. For example, the Drybrook Sandstone is 350 feet thick in the Wigpool area but towards Chepstow it thins out to about seventy feet.

The Devonian Rocks are mainly red sandstones derived from the erosion of a vast continent lying to the north of Britain some 395 million years ago. These deposits were sediments laid down in lakes, inland seas, deltas and desert plains, the climate at the time being hot with a long dry season. This can be inferred because, in tropical regions of the world today where there is a long season, the waste rock tends to be red with a deposit known laterite. Red oxides of iron colour the land surface and the Old Red Sandstone rocks are mainly composed of sand grains (quartz) coated with iron oxide in the same way. These conditions continued for some fifty

The Rocks and How They Were Formed

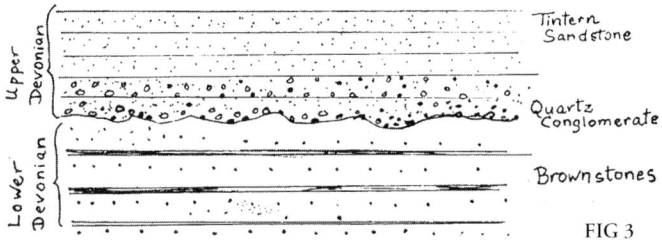

FIG 3

The unconformity between the Upper and Lower Devonian is marked by the Quartz Conglomerate. This type of unconformity is known as a NON-SEQUENCE because the strata of Lower and Upper Devonian are both horizontal as if there had been no long interval of time between the two.

million years, during which time vast amounts of sands, gravels and lake muds accumulated to a total thickness of some 3,500 feet.

During the later part of the Devonian period, earth movements occurred which folded the Old Red Sandstone into mountains and, after erosion of this land surface, the waste rock in the form of gravels and screes covered the surface to form the Quartz Conglomerate. More sands deposited on this formed the Tintern Sandstone of the Upper Devonian period. These rocks vary from red to yellow in colour and have an average thickness of some 400 feet. The diagram, Figure 3, explains how the Quartz Conglomerate separates the upper and lower divisions of the Devonian rocks. This is known as an unconformity, and between these two sets of rocks there is a long interval of time when the Lower Devonian rocks were eroded. Figure 3 shows that both sets of strata dip at the same angle but the conglomerate at the base of the Upper Devonian separates them and this type of unconformity does not show the usual contrast in dips between the two sets of rocks. In other places there is a marked angular unconformity between the Lower and Upper as shown in Figure 6 in the next chapter. The Quartz Conglomerate is a very resistant rock made hard by the numerous quartz pebbles in the matrix of sandstone; the local term, 'pudding stone' is very apt indeed. Although only about 100 feet thick, it forms a marked relief feature almost encircling the saucer-like basin of the Forest of Dean and giving rise to pretty wooded scarps, often with bare crags of conglomerate.

The Devonian period is termed the Age of Fishes because at this time in the history of the earth the early vertebrates appeared in lakes, rivers and seas all over the world. Fishes arrived first on scene in the Ordovician period, to be followed millions of years later by amphibia, reptiles and mammals. We have the first fossil record of trees in the Devonian period but plants were very primitive, colonising the land areas with rather thin vegetation. Here was a new environment just waiting for occupation by the reptiles.

The Devonian period came to an end some 345 million years ago and the semi-arid continent began to sink beneath the sea. It was a clear sea because, on account of the surrounding arid lands, few large rivers flowed into it. This was the beginning of the Carboniferous period and in these seas lived corals, crinoids (sea lilies) and brachiopods in great abundance. Their remains were laid down to form layers of limestone over which dominate the topography in the Wye valley at Symond's Yat and in the Chepstow area. These limestones vary a good deal from a white oolite to the pinkish grey of the dolomite. Later, the sea became sandy with more active rivers because of the rising land areas and so the Drybrook Sandstone was deposited. This is not the equivalent of the famous Millstone Grit that overlies the limestones of the Pennines and from the table we see that the sandstone forms part of the Carboniferous Limestone series, and is rather well developed in the Dean area. Farther south, this sandstone thins out and passes into quite a thick limestone, the Drybrook Limestone. The Drybrook Sandstone indicates the change from clear to sandy seas at the time. This series of rocks belongs the Lower Carboniferous period which lasted twenty million years and came to an end when all the strata were folded and eroded, so again we have a long interval of time before all the succeeding sandstones, shales and coal seams of the Upper Coal Measures were laid down. The geographical conditions in this part of Britain at the time were similar to those of the tropical deltas of the world today, eg the deltas of the Amazon and Ganges, but of course the dense vegetation of 250 million years ago consisted of trees which we could hardly recognise today. The rapid burial of these swamp forests by vast quantities of sand and mud is one of the most important factors in the formation of coal, a fact well demonstrated in the numerous quarries in the Pennant Sandstone of the central part of Dean. When one realises that the total thickness of the Upper

Coal Measures in the area is over a thousand feet, one can understand why the centre of the coal basin in the Forest of Dean is an area of high relief caused by the outcrop of these massive sandstones.

At the end of the Carboniferous period, 270 million years ago, another period of earth movements occurred, but this time it was on a very large scale and affected a good deal of the continent of Europe. When strata are heaved up into folds it is obvious that mountains will be formed and this process of mountain building is termed 'orogeny' and this particular one is called the Hercynian orogeny. Vast chains of mountains were formed, which stretched from Southern Ireland, South Wales, Cornwall, Devon, Brittany, the Massif Central, Vosges and Black Forest to the mountains of Czechoslovakia. In fact, all these highland areas are just the eroded stumps of the ancient Hercynian mountains. The Forest of Dean and Wye Valley regions were once mountains of massive limestones, probably resembling the Dinaric Alps in Jugoslavia today. The humid conditions of the Coal Measure swamp forests now came to an end and limestone ranges loomed up over the semi-arid plains of the Permian and Triassic periods. The climatic conditions seem to indicate a return to the Devonian times with long hot dry seasons and high temperatures in which the Upper Coal Measures ere being eroded away and vast desert plains covered with red deposits began to form. Thus Triassic rocks, like the Devonian, are red with iron oxide, eg the Keuper Marl, a Triassic rock which is very familiar to farmers in the Midlands and also to civil engineers who have to construct new motorways through it.

Limestone screes formed at the foot of the mountains and today we can see these in the deposits known as the Dolomitic Conglomerate which, in places, can be seen resting on the upturned edges of the Carboniferous Limestones in the Chepstow area. Although called a conglomerate, in this region the limestone fragments found mixed up in the red marl are very angular, so that the term Dolomitic Breccia would be more apt. This rock forms the base of the Triassic rocks in this region. It is in fissures filled with these scree deposits that the first fossil remains of mammals in Britain were found in the Mendips. They were very small rat-sized creatures, probably marsupials of nocturnal habit because the world at that time was dominated by the reptiles. The hitherto unoccupied land areas of the world were then invaded by all kinds of reptiles, the most successful being the dinosaurs. The beginnings of this invasion occurred in the Coal Measure swamps and the next 200 million years, the Mesozoic era, is known as the Age of Reptiles. This completes our short summary of the rocks found in the west of Dean and Wye Valley and it can now be seen that part of the history of the earth is exemplified here. It is a sequence of the following:

1. Deposits laid down to form sedimentary rocks.
2. Earth upheaved and the rocks folded—period of orogeny.
3. Erosion of the mountains formed in 2.
4. Cycle repeated again as more sediments are laid down on the eroded stumps of the mountains.

This has been repeated at intervals in the last 1,000 million years but, as yet, there is no generally accepted explanation of the causes of these upheavals in the earth's crust, although some geologists assert they have been caused by periodic movements deep down in the earth's mantle. We can also conclude from this short summary that the fossiliferous rocks in Dean would be in the limestones formed in coral seas and a great wealth of fossil plant remains would be in the Coal Measures. Fossils in the red beds of the Devonian and Trias are difficult to find and the reasons for this will be explained later.

Chapter 3

The Main Structures of the Region

WE are now in a position to examine the geological map of the area. Figure 4, on page 20. If this were a coloured map, rocks of the same age would be printed in the same colour, as on the Geological Survey maps, and all who want to study the rocks of the area should purchase the geological map of the Monmouth area. Sheet No 233 and the adjoining Chepstow Sheet, No 250. These coloured maps on a scale of one inch to the mile represent many years of field work done by officers of the Geological Survey.

The sketch map, Figure 4, does not show all the series belonging to the Carboniferous Limestone or the Upper Coal Measures; for this, a scale of six inches to the mile would be necessary. On further inspection it will be seen that some outcrops, eg the Carboniferous Limestone series, vary in width and Figure 5 illustrates this feature. It is obvious that when the slope of the strata, referred to now as the dip, is steep, there is a narrow outcrop over the ground, and when the dip is gentle a wide outcrop results. From this it is also apparent that variations in relief, such as hills and valleys, will also control the outcrop of strata. Another important feature of the map is termed overstep and the best example is in the Lydney area where the Coal Measure rocks, which usually rest on the upturned edges of the Carboniferous Limestone series, rest on Devonian rocks and so conceal the limestones below. This happens between Lydney and Danby Lodge (a few miles north of Blakeney) and is explained in Figure 6. This overstep is due to an unconformity between two groups of rocks and represents a long interval of time compared with that taken for the usual rate of sedimentation. The arrows on the map indicate the general direction of dip which varies considerably as the strata were much disturbed during the great Hercynian orogeny. Finally, it should be noted that the river Wye ignores the strata and flows across them. No matter whether the rocks are hard or soft, it pushes relentlessly on and this curious phenomenon calls for an explanation which is given in a special chapter on the Wye Valley.

The Forest of Dean and Wye Valley provide a great contrast to the Cotswolds where the Jurassic strata are only gently inclined to the south-east at an angle of dip of just a few degrees. In Dean, the strata are very much disturbed and this can be related to three periods of orogeny viz:

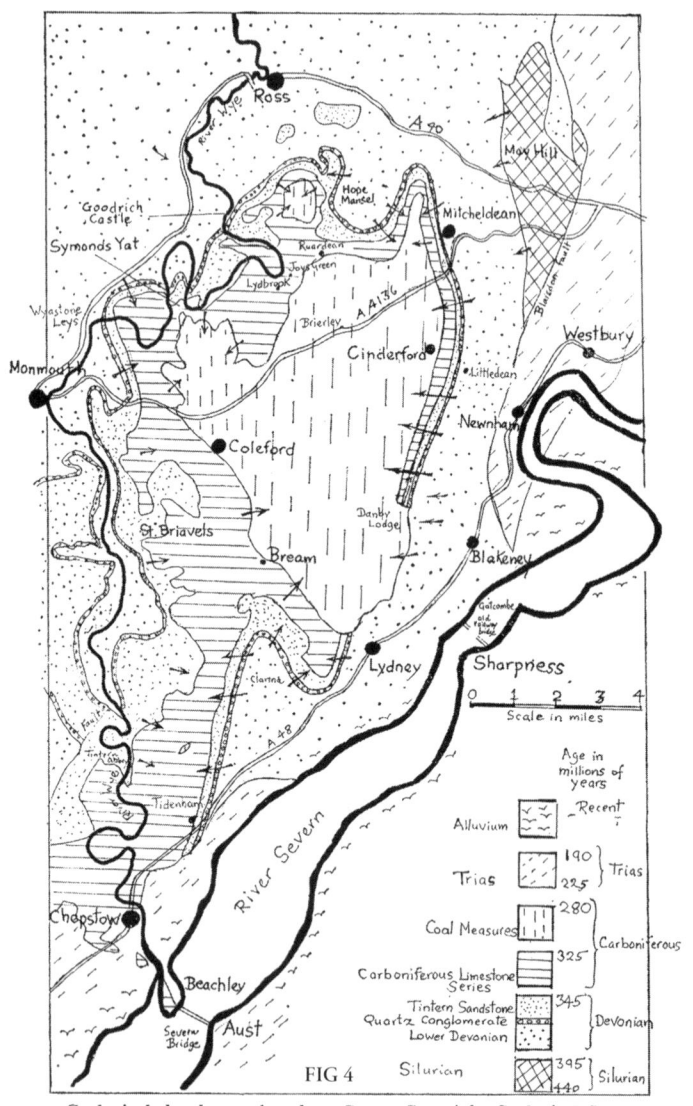

Geological sketch map based on Crown Copyright Geological Survey map by permission of the Controller of H.M. Stationery Office

The Main Structures of the Region

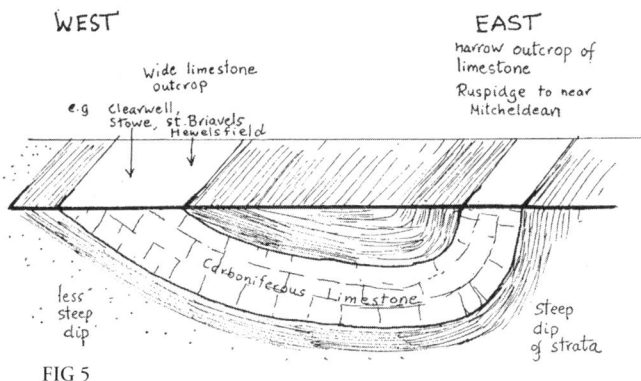

FIG 5

Diagram explaining how the dip controls the outcrop. Of course the relief is not flat as shown above

1. Intra Devonian orogeny
   —370 million years BP.
2. Intra Carboniferous orogeny
   —325 million years BP.
3. The main Hercynian orogeny
   —280 million years BP.

(Note that geologists use the term BP, meaning 'before the present'.)

It was this last upheaval that really formed the structures of the region, and the scenery as we see it today is the result of subsequent erosion. One must remember that the earth's crust is always in a state of movement and at intervals reaches a climax in an intense period of mountain building. Figure 7 shows the spacing of these periods in a diagrammatic form. These disturbances of the earth's crust occur along the lines of the ancient cracked pavement which are termed 'mobile belts' and the Malvern Axis could be related to a line of weakness which has exerted considerable influence throughout the Palaeozoic era in the Dean area. Figure 8A shows this axis with its system of nearly parallel folds trending in a northerly direction across the Forest, and in general to the west of the Malvern north-south line. When rocks come up against resistance in underlying structures they are deflected, forced into folds and wrap round the obstacles. This can be demonstrated when we push a tablecloth under which we have placed a few books. The folds in the cloth will produce a pattern controlled by the books underneath. Figures 8A and 8B

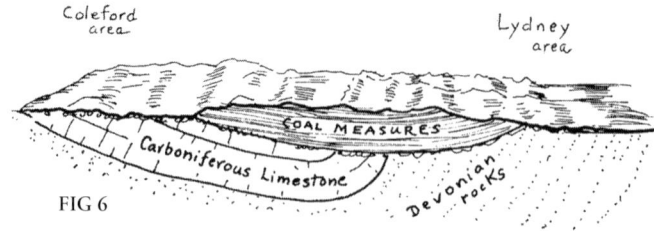

FIG 6

Owing to the intra-Carboniferous folding the Coal Measures rest on Devonian rocks in the Lydney to Danby Lodge area but at Coleford and the western areas of Dean the Coal Measures rest on the upturned edges of the Carboniferous series.

show how a system of folds arranged 'en echelon' have been developed on the western side of the Malvern Line. Some folds trend NW while others exhibit a NE trend. In North Wales and Scotland this NE trend is a well recognised structural line termed Caledonian and it occurred during a great period of orogeny at the end of the Silurian period some 395 million years ago. It can be seen from the map above that the Lower Severn Axis has a Caledonian trend but it is believed that movement along this line also occurred in the Later Carboniferous period.

It was during the Hercynian period of earth movements that the main downfold or syncline of the Forest of Dean basin was formed.

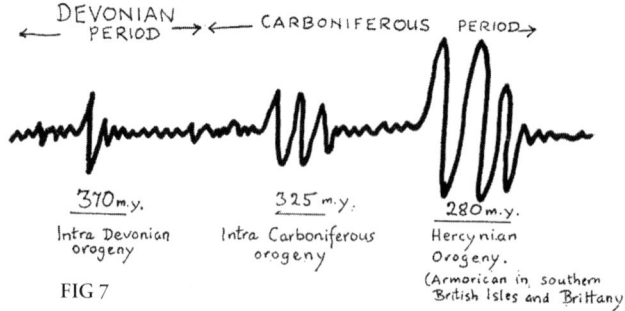

FIG 7

Diagram showing time intervals for periods of OROGENY, when Earth movements reached a climax

The Main Structures of the Region

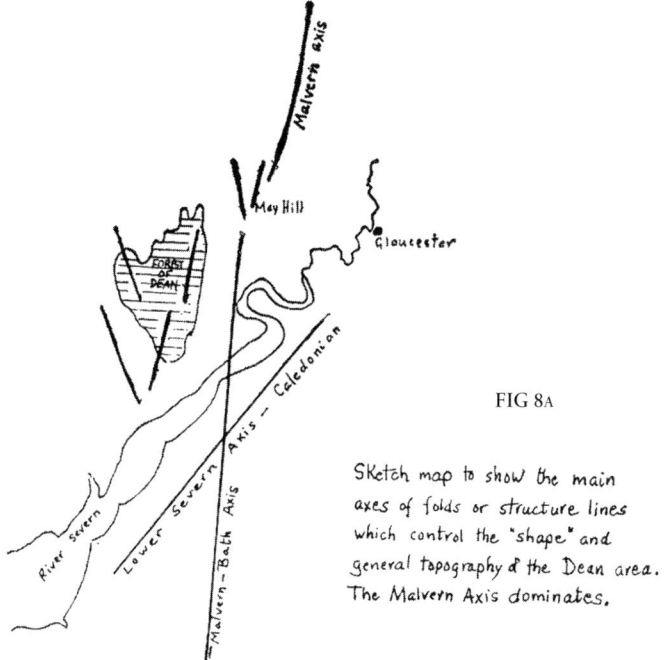

FIG 8A

Sketch map to show the main axes of folds or structure lines which control the "shape" and general topography of the Dean area. The Malvern Axis dominates.

Figure 9A shows how the dips are very steep on the eastern limb of the fold and only gently inclined on the west. Figure 9B shows how much of the scenery which we see today is due to erosion. In general, we can expect to find the highest points in the area somewhere on the rim of the saucer. In fact, our highest point is at Ruardean Hill at 951 feet on the northern rim of the syncline. The block diagram, Figure 10, is an attempt to show both strata and structures influencing the general topography in Dean. It clearly shows the hard rocks reared up into ridges and scarps and indicates how the topography in Dean is influenced by the underlying structure.

The Malvern Axis can be traced south to Bath where the hot springs may be related to it. Where this axis crosses the Severn near sharpness there are cliffs of Devonian rocks on either side which also outcrop on the river bed. This gave railway engineers a suitable site where the harder Devonian rocks afforded a

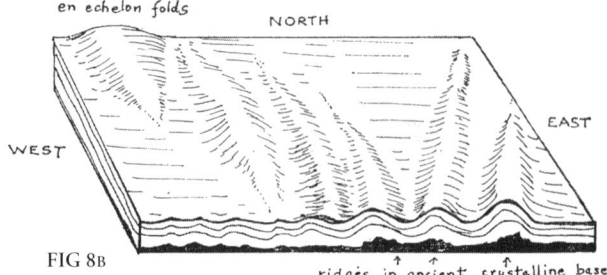

FIG 8B

Diagram to show how folds in strata can change direction which is partly controlled by resistant ridges in the underlying basement. These folds are periclines and are arranged 'en echelon'

good foundation for the piers of a rail bridge constructed in 1874—a wonderful feat for its time. Another good bridging point is between Beachley and Aust where three folds converge, viz the Beachley-Clanna pericline (a pericline is a dome-shaped fold), the Tidenham syncline and the Chepstow anticline. These structures bring the Carboniferous rocks up to the bed of the river Severn and civil engineers took advantage of this between 1960 and 1966 when constructing the magnificent Severn bridge. The towers, 450 feet high, rest on a hard basement of Carboniferous Limestone rocks, and the approach roads on either side are cuttings in soft deposits of the Keuper Marl of Triassic age, which posed new problems in rock mechanics for the builders of motorways.

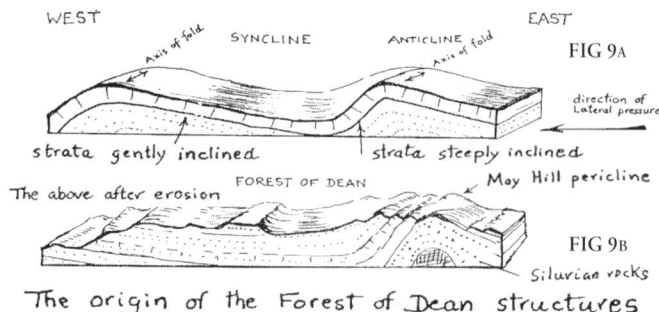

The origin of the Forest of Dean structures

The Main Structures of the Region

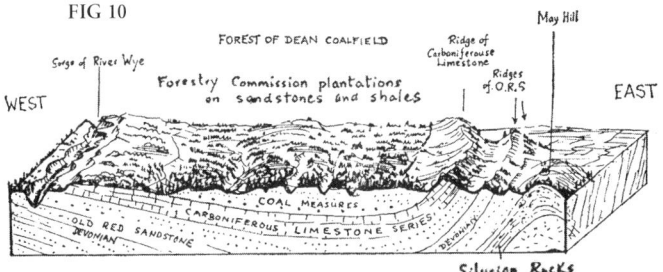

Simplified block diagram of the Forest of Dean Syncline showing how it occupies a basin in the Old Red Sandstone. (Devonian)

Although to a geologist the Severn is a recent river, having originated partly as a spillway from the melting ice sheet that lay across the Midlands some 50,000 years ago, its general direction is controlled by this 'revived' Caledonian axis. This Lower Severn Axis has had much influence on the kinds of sedimentation on either side of it during the Carboniferous period, and from the map it seems that its convergence with the Malvern Line in the Sharpness area not only gives our first bridging point but creates a kind of step on the bed of the river Severn which is said by experts to be one of the causes of the Severn Bore.

The sketch map over shows the main structural features of the area, but many of the faults are omitted for the sake of simplicity. Faults, which are cracks in the rocks along which movement has taken place, are of great importance to miners but they have not affected the landscape in Dean to any extent. There is a tendency for folds to be less parallel to the Malvern Line in the Chepstow area where they trend more to the north-west. They are coming under the influence of an east-west line of folding which is very common in South-west Ireland, the Mendips, South-west England and Brittany. A Breton name given to this type of Hercynian folding is Armorican.

To sum up, the main groups of folds in the region are:

1. The main basin of the Dean area—the main syncline.
2. The Wigpool syncline.
3. The Hope Mansel dome.
4. The Staple Edge monocline.
5. The Worcester syncline.
6. The Beachley-Clanna pericline.
7. The Tidenham syncline.
8. The Chepstow anticline.

In later chapters, these areas will be studied in greater detail.

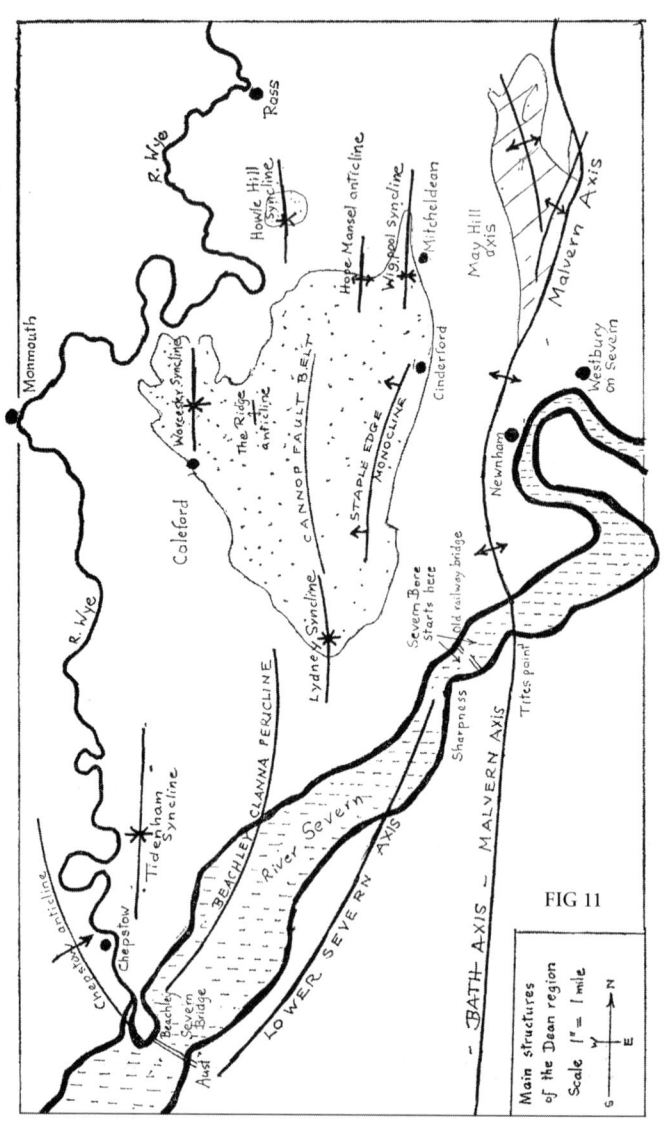

FIG 11

Chapter 4

A Traverse of the Dean Syncline

THIS chapter is devoted to the visitor who would like to get an overall picture of the region in a single day trip. A special Journey across the northern section from east to west has been selected, in which the main structures and rock types may be clearly seen. In which the main structures and rock types may be clearly seen. In its structure the Forest of Dean is a unique region, an interior plateau in the form of an oval-shaped saucer floored with Carboniferous Limestones, the central portion being infilled with Coal Measure shales and sandstones. Generally speaking, in a geographical sense, plateau areas throughout the world tend to be rather isolated regions in which the inhabitants develop customs and dialects of their own. The Forest is no exception and although its isolation is being broken down by motorways and bus services, the inhabitants still preserve clannish characteristics.

To a traveller approaching from Gloucester, following the A40 to Ross-on-Wye, the dome-shaped mass of May Hill dominates the skyline. The range of hills of which May Hill is the central point forms a continuation of the Malvern Line of folding and this anticlinal structure of Silurian rocks must be crossed in order to enter our area. It is usual to find an upfold adjacent to a downfold, so that the May Hill anticline is complementary to the Dean syncline, the latter being a much larger feature. The descent from the ridge is at Longhope, where the region of Lower Devonian rocks begins. This becomes evident when we notice that most of the older buildings and churches are built of Old Red Sandstone, just as in the Cotswolds the local Oolite stone has for centuries been he main building material. The landscape now assumes quite a different character from the scarplands of Gloucestershire, for here occur the strong north-south ridges, three of which must be crossed before we reach the outer wall of Dean. The ridges are made of hard bands of massive red sandstones belonging to a group of rocks known as the Brownstones, but the name does not tally with the colour here.

The strata are superbly displayed in the Wilderness Quarry on Breakheart Hill (Figure 12) where they have been heaved up to an angle of 60 degrees to the horizontal, a very impressive reminder of the enormous forces within the earth's crust which build mountains. This is an active quarry exporting a red rockery stone much favoured for

FIG 12

Wilderness Quarry, Mitcheldean
Lower Devonian sandstones and shales dipping 60° W

paving slabs and building, some loads going as far afield as Kent. On closer inspection, preferably in bright sunshine, the sandstone will be seen to sparkle with a flaky mineral called muscovite, a variety of mica. The crystals have what mineralogists call a strong basal cleavage, and their parallel orientation makes it very easy for the rock to split along and parallel to the bedding planes, thus giving us our useful flagstones. The rocks are red because the quartz grains in the sandstone are coated with a red iron oxide, haematite, but in places chemical changes have given rise to a ferrous oxide which produces a grey-green, mottled colouring. Some of the sandstones are interbedded with shales which, after rainy days, produce a sticky, chocolate-coloured mud which makes it impossible to operate machines, so that we may find the men working on a Sunday to take advantage of dry weather. Occasionally, geologists have found fish remains in the shales, and even in a brief stay one can see fossil sun cracks on the great bedding planes, especially on the shaly, grey green slabs. These polygon-like patterns are the result of hot sunshine drying up lake muds 400 million years ago.

After crossing two more ridges we are on the outskirts of Mitcheldean, which lies at the foot of 'the great wall' of the Forest but still on the Devonian sandstones. The block diagram Figure 13 shows the next and most important part of our journey, up the steep incline to the Point Inn situated right on the Quartz Conglomerate, an outcrop of which may be seen just ten yards from the inn door (Figure 14). On the hillside above the main road, just before we reach the inn, there are large tumbled blocks of the conglomerate, some weighing about a hundred tons and seeming to threaten the houses below. This resistant rock can be examined in detail just by the inn where white quartz pebbles of this pudding stone are very conspicuous, especially after rain. The pebbles are stratified in a hard sandstone matrix and more details about this rock will be found in the chapter on Symond's Yat. Meanwhile, we should note what great strength is added to our west of Dean 'rampart' by this pudding stone. A small stream has breached the rocks here forming a small ravine, and although the present stream is insignificant, in the past, when the climate was wetter, it must have been quite a torrent to have sculptured such a deep valley.

We now come to a series of quarries on Plump Hill, made famous because they are mentioned in all the geological literature on Dean (Figure 15). This is a popular area for geological studies but the quarries are fast disappearing as they are now used for dumping town refuse. In fact, very little can be now seen of our first quarry which is in the lowest division of the Carboniferous Limestone series,

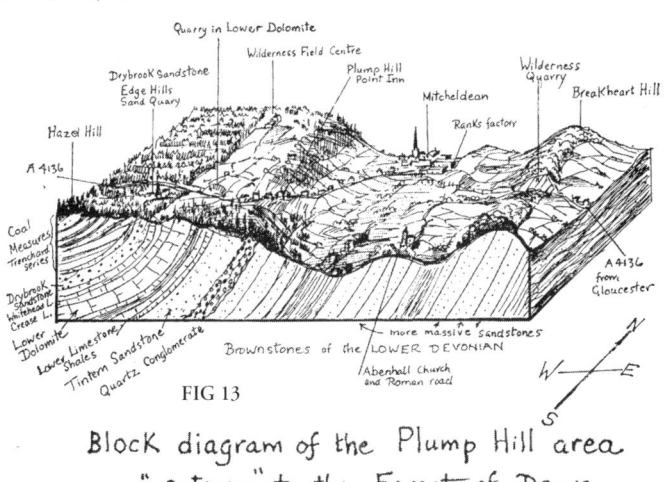

FIG 13

Block diagram of the Plump Hill area "gateway" to the Forest of Dean.

FIG 14

POINT INN, PLUMP HILL on the outcrop of the Quartz Conglomerate

the Lower Limestone Shale. This is only a hundred yards up the road from the Point Inn but masses of refuse almost obliterate the thinly bedded limestones and shales. Close by, but with some difficulty, can be seen the actual junction of the Devonian and Carboniferous rocks. The red Tintern Sandstones of the Upper Devonian come up against the crinoidal limestones of the Carboniferous without any angular unconformity.

Almost adjoining this quarry is a fine exposure of the Lower Dolomite, the quarry entrance being on the roadside. At first sight it seems as though the rocks are dipping in an unexpected direction and this is because the joints are a much stronger feature than the bedding planes. The sketch, Figure 16, shows how the true dip of the strata is revealed on the cliff top, being inclined at 60 degrees to the west as in the Wilderness Quarry. Recognition of dolomite rock presents some difficulty to inexperienced students of geology but the main features of this type of limestone are shown here. In colour, it is pinkish grey due to staining with haematite, but where well exposed to the weather at the cliff top, it changes to buff colour—a chemical change set up by the hydration of the haematite to the brown mineral limonite. Also at the cliff top can be seen rather peculiar weathering resembling decayed bones, hence the term 'carious weathering'.

Dolomite is a mineral, and a rock almost entirely made of this is called a dolomitic limestone. It is a double carbonate of magnesium and calcium and therefore tends to erode in a different way from a pure limestone. Closer examination of the rock in this quarry shows the texture to be sugary or saccharoidal. A good hand-lens will reveal the sugar-like grains to be tiny, rhomb-shaped crystals of dolomite. The tall excavators of the nearby Edge Hills Sand Quarry now attract our attraction, and here can be seen the yellow-brown sandstone cliffs of the Drybrook Sandstone, the highest division of the Carboniferous Limestone series in Dean. It is a very colourful rock, often stained red brown with haematite, and close to the quarry entrance there is the old iron mine shaft excavated by the miners to a depth of 550 feet in 1837. The sandstone is soft enough in places to be crushed into a good building sand but interbedded shales create much waste, and quarries of this sandstone in other areas have had to be abandoned because of the shaly or conglomeratic character of the rock.

At the summit of Plump Hill we can look westwards across the Dean coal basin dotted with tip heaps of old collieries, and beyond to the Wye valley and the western rim of the saucer where the Devonian rocks come to the surface again. Our aim now is to cross the basin to the rim on the other side, near Upper Lydbrook. The presence of Coal Measure rocks is indicated by Meering Pond which lies very close to Edge Hills Quarry. Ponds, streams, springs and marshy ground seem to occur at the junction of the Coal Measures and Carboniferous Limestone series because much water is released to the surface due to the presence of underlying Coal Measure clays and shales. The underground water is often released at the surface where the shales prevent water from penetrating any deeper. The route downhill to Nailbridge almost follows the

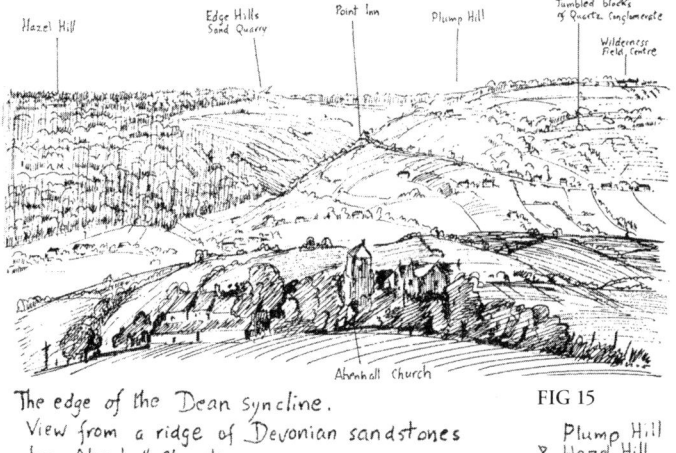

The edge of the Dean syncline.
View from a ridge of Devonian sandstones by Abenhall Church

FIG 15
Plump Hill & Hazel Hill

westward dip slope of the Pennant Sandstone, which is here at about 20 degrees. Holy Trinity Church, standing conspicuously on the slopes of Harry Hill, is a good example of the use of the grey Pennant stone of which the old houses in the locality are also built—in striking contrast to the cottages of red sandstone at Longhope. Here and there among the trees can be seen small dumps of blue-grey shale revealing the presence of small coal pits. Fossil plants can be found in these shales, as in many of the pit heaps of coal mines. At Nailbridge we can get a good idea of the type of rock which occupies the central basin, for dotted all over the hillsides are many old quarries in the Pennant Sandstone, every exposure showing nearly the same dip of about 20 degrees, although here it is southwards as we are now in the northern rim of the basin. Only twenty yards from the door of the Railway Inn, Nailbridge, there is an excellent quarry face of this rock, another repetition of 'rocks by the wayside' we saw at Point Inn. (Figure 17.)

Continuing westwards on the A4136 we pass the huge man-made mountain of waste from the old Northern United Colliery which closed down in 1965. Permission should be obtained from the caretaker to roam over this vast tip heap of Coal Measure shales and sandstones, where one can find good specimens of fossil plants in the

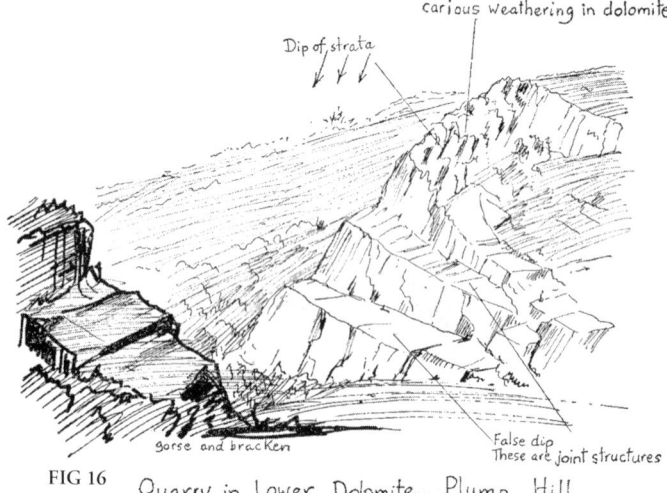

FIG 16 Quarry in Lower Dolomite, Plump Hill

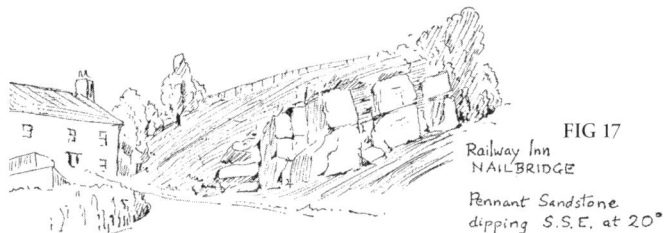

FIG 17
Railway Inn
NAILBRIDGE

Pennant Sandstone
dipping S.S.E. at 20°

form of fragments of tree trunks, some even showing impressions of the leaf scars (Figure 18). Many of the rock fragments have a distinct red colour, due to the spontaneous combustion that often starts up inside the mound. Erosion proceeds very rapidly in this unconsolidated material, and efforts are being made to retard the downhill creep of shale by planting trees. For the next few miles the scenery is somewhat monotonous and rather closed in by the dense pine forests on both sides of the road. In the clearings, bracken rather than grass rapidly colonises the acid soils so that sheep deprived of good grass tend to graze by the roadside. At Brierley, old quarries and tip heaps afford more open country from which we can appreciate the plateau-like nature of the landscape, which is best seen about half a mile past the inn at Brierley. The block diagram, Figure 19, shows the fine scenic effect of valleys deeply eroded into the Coal Measure sandstones. The Greathough valley between Astonbridge Hill Inclosure and Barnedge Hill is well worth visiting.

FIG 18

A man made "mountain"
Waste rock from Northern United Colliery near Nailbridge

Geology Explained in the Forest of Dean and Wye Valley

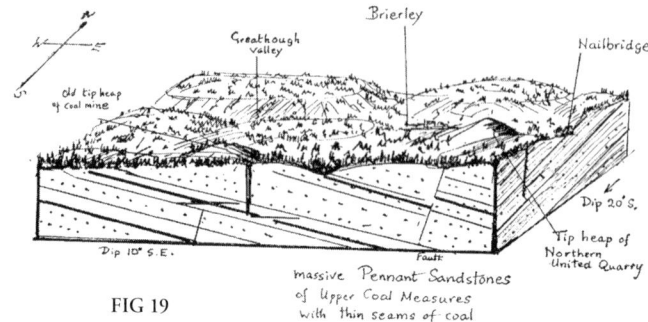

FIG 19

Plateau like country in the Pennant Sandstones with deep valleys.

The A4136 road must now be left as we turn to Upper Lydbrook, making use of a deep tributary valley which joins the Wye at Lower Lydbrook. Turning off to the right at Joy's Green, we come now to the western rim of the saucer. The block diagram, figure 20, indicates the structural reasons for the very impressive scenery. The housing estate of Joy's Green lies perched on a foundation of massive Lower Dolomite which is now tilted at 20 degrees in the opposite direction to the strata at Plump Hill (Figure 21). Here is a wonderful example of strong geological control over the planning of a housing estate, for the houses look down on one another and across the valley to the great hillside mass of the Coal Measures. On one side is a hill of the Carboniferous Limestone series and, on the other, a much higher hill formed of the Coal Measure rocks scarred with many quarries in the Pennant Sandstone, gleaming like castle walls in the afternoon sunshine. This scene is the finest in the region for demonstrating the double rim of the Dean syncline. In the quarries near Joy's Green Post Office the massive sandstones, often with bedding planes ten feet apart, show on their under surfaces the casts of large tree trunks 280 million years old. This rock has strongly developed vertical joints which have made quarrying quite easy and have produced the castle-like wall effect in the cliff face. The writer once watched some children of Joy's Green playing at castles in this natural type of adventure playground.

Horse Lea Hill (see block diagram, Figure 20) has a gentle slope for the Trenchard series of the Coal Measures and a much steeper slope higher up caused by the outcropping

34

A Traverse of the Dean Syncline

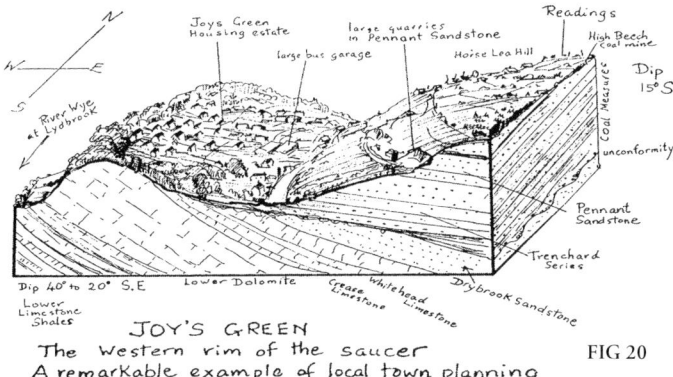

FIG 20

JOY'S GREEN
The Western rim of the saucer
A remarkable example of local town planning

Pennant Sandstone, but everywhere bracken seems to take over the open spaces except where there are pine forests. The hill reaches a height of 800 feet and excellent views of the Wye valley can be obtained from the summit. Inside the hill, and buried under the sandstones of the Pennant, is the famous Coleford High Delf coal seam which is still being mined not far away at High Beech.

We have now completed our traverse from Plump Hill to Joy's Green and it will have demonstrated the importance to scenery of both rock type and structure. The return journey should be made on the same route as the view from a different direction will help to strengthen the notion that the study of rocks and scenery are inseparable.

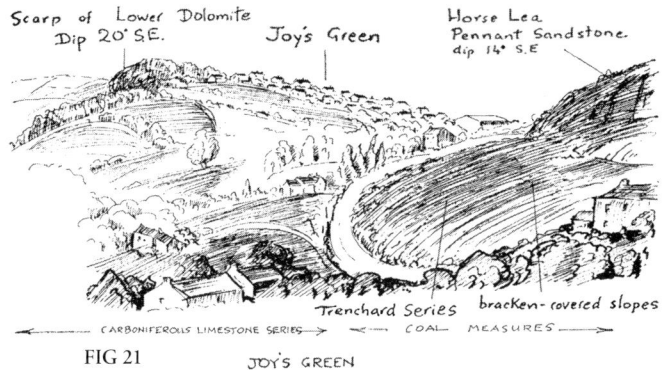

FIG 21   JOY'S GREEN

Chapter 5
The Littledean and Ruspidge Areas

IF we compare the geological and topographical maps of the Dean region, we see that there is a distinct scarp stretching from the north near Lea, southwards to Blakeney, and that there are only three breaks in this 'wall', at Plump Hill, Littledean and Soudley. Only one of these, the Soudley Gap, is in the form of a river valley leading into Dean, the other two being easier road routes climbing up over the upturned edges of the Carboniferous and Devonian rocks. In the days of horse transport, this north-south scarp presented quite a formidable obstacle but motor transport has made the region easily accessible and revealed its great attractions to new residents and tourists.

The village of Littledean can be reached by turning off from the A48 Chepstow road at Elton, a few miles past Westbury-on-Severn, on to the A4125 to Cinderford. There is no need even to consult a geological map after the ten-mile journey from Gloucester over the low-lying country of the Severn Vale floored by Keuper Marl (Trias) for there is a sudden rise by Pope's Hill only a mile or two from the turn where we again enter the country of the Brownstones of the Lower Devonian series. This is a land of deep valleys separated by steep ridges, where

The Gaol, Littledean
built in 1790 of Old Red Sandstone
with window faces of Pennant Sandstone.

FIG 22

FIG 23
Block diagram of the Littledean area

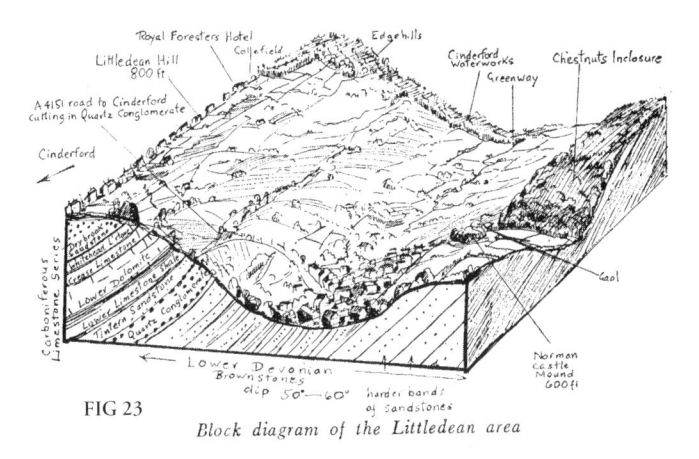

most of the old cottages and barns built of the local Old Red Sandstone indicate the geology, as in the Longhope region. One of the finest examples of architecture in this stone is the old gaol situated south-east of Littledean, close to a gap in a Red Sandstone ridge forming the high ground of Chestnuts Inclosure. An old quarry by the roadside some twenty yards away probably provided the stone for this prison, which was built in 1790 as a 'house of correction'. The old records indicate that the inmates were often poachers and vagrants from the Forest but today it is used as the local police court. Geologists should visit the building to see how appropriately the massive sandstone blocks were used in building the ten-foot high walls. Figure 22 shows part of the general design. Detailed examination of the walls shows that the blocks have weathered considerably in the last 180 years, especially on the sides much exposed to the sun. The flaking is caused by the heating and cooling of the surface layers. Although it is a slow process, only about a quarter of an inch having fallen away since 1790, it is accelerated by the abundant flaky mica in the rock.

The block diagram, Figure 23, has been drawn from the excellent viewpoint on Castle Mound, the site of a Norman castle, from which the spire of Mitcheldean church can be seen in the distance, for both Mitcheldean and Littledean occupy the northern and southern ends of the structural valley formed in softer shaly sandstone dipping

50 to 60 degrees westwards. The guest house in Littledean is becoming quite a rendezvous for many British geologists as the village is an excellent field centre for Dean. The steepest part of the hill on the Cinderford side of Littledean is due to the outcrop of the Quartz Conglomerate which is well exposed in a roadside cutting and easily detected by the gleaming white quartz pebbles. Along the hillside it can be traced by the rough grazing and general gorse cover for the outcrop of this resistant rock is never ploughed. The top of the hill is just on the outskirts of Cinderford and this part of our natural rampart is called Littledean Hill. From the Royal Foresters Hotel can be seen one of the finest views in the whole area. The scene in front, depicted in Figure 24, shows the great meander of the river Severn at Newnham. The May Hill-Malvern Axis may have something to do with this

FIG 24   *Dean Hill from Royal Foresters Hotel*

great deflection of the Severn. One of the ridges connected with this axis can be seen in front, with Chestnuts Inclosure on the left and the Norman Castle Mound to the right (Figure 25). The gap in the sandstone ridge obviously accounts for the geographical situation of Littledean, which appears to command the entrance to Dean. Most people know of the famous panoramic view from Pleasant Stile on the Newnham road showing the whole bend of the river uninterrupted by any ridge (Figure 26), but the writer prefers the view from the Royal Foresters Hotel because it so clearly demonstrates how the ridges seem to guide the course of the Severn. What finer place than this spot for a geography lesson for children who can learn something about the location of towns, and at the same

The Littledean and Ruspidge Areas

FIG 25

Littledean from Dean Hill

time correlate the view before them with an ordinary atlas map showing this great Severn meander?

Northwards from the Royal Foresters Hotel the top of the scarp extends into the thickly wooded area of Edgehills at a general elevation of 800 feet. Rather an eyesore close to the hotel is a huge dump from the old St Annal's iron-mine shaft which was sunk to a depth of 687 feet. Most of the top of this scarp is of the Drybrook Sandstone which is here rather ferruginous (rich in iron), but the main iron-ore bodies are in the Crease Limestone at the bottom of the shaft. There are two exposures of this sandstone in old quarries on the way to Edgehills. Although the first is only a small one beside the Forest Road, it displays beds of conglomerate which are annoying features to quarry workers who require the softer sandstone beds for crushing into sand. In the second quarry, lower down the hill,

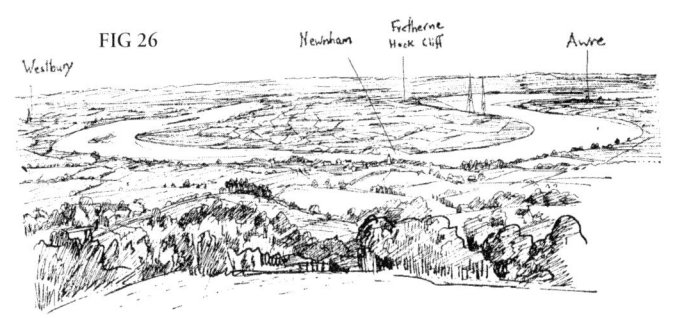

FIG 26

Pleasant Stile: the great meander bed in the River Severn

FIG 27

Old quarry in Drybrook Sandstone showing ridges of conglomerate and shale

can be seen two upturned edges of conglomerate and shaly sandstone with trench-like excavations cut out as the men worked into the softer beds. Figure 27 shows the steeply inclined bedding planes which rather hampered the quarry work.

In some of the blue grey shales the uppermost bedding planes are covered with branching structures resembling worm casts. It must be remembered that the Drybrook Sandstone is a marine sediment and some worm-like animals have left these traces, a particular type of 'chondrites' as they are called by palaeontologists. Similar trace fossils are visible in the same sandstone formation at Upper Lydbrook and at Puddlebrook Quarry.

Moving downhill, we observe that the sequence of strata is the same as at Plump Hill but that the outcrops are at different levels (Figure 28). Just below the old sandstone quarry in amongst the trees can be seen groups of very deep holes, the more dangerous ones wired in to prevent sheep from falling in. These are old shallow workings for iron ore in the Crease Limestone which provide much interest for pot-holing and caving societies. The general term for this type of terrain is 'scowles' and more will be said about these in a later chapter on iron mining.

Water was a problem in these mines and here a powerful stream from above had to be led away from the workings by a specially constructed, stone-lined aqueduct which can still be seen below the sandstone quarry. On the way to the Cinderford Waterworks below, we pass a cliff face of the pinkish-grey Lower Dolomite and, after passing a pebble-strewn path indicating the Quartz Conglomerate outcrop, we come to the pumping station at Green Bottom. This was constructed in 1880 and has two wells, 168 and 124 feet in depth, from which water is pumped up to a reservoir near the Royal Foresters Hotel to provide sufficient head.

Both the Drybrook and Devonian sandstone formations are important natural storage reservoirs as water is

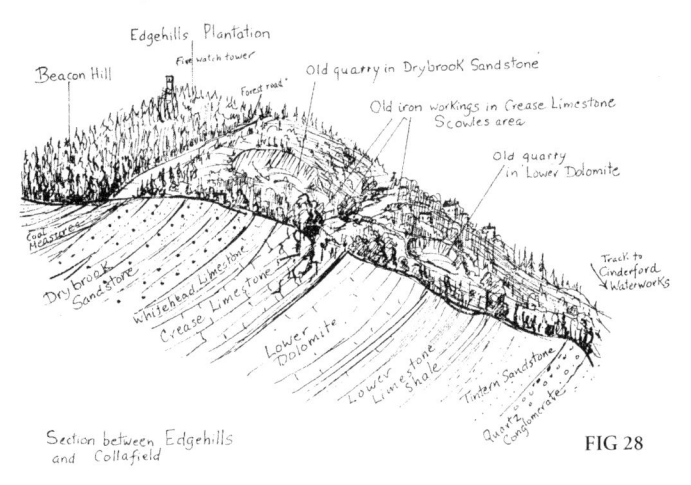

FIG 28

Section between Edgehills and Collafield

held in the spaces between the sand grains. The famous St Anthony's Well nearby seems to work in sympathy with the wells here.

The Ruspidge area is in Dean proper for it is located on the other side of the scarp just south of Cinderford. On weekdays, the noise of Shakemantle Quarry attracts our attention and it is well worth a visit to see the highly-inclined strata of the Lower Dolomite being excavated for road aggregate. The exposed surfaces of the bedding planes are matched by those in the large Drybrook Sandstone Quarry on the opposite side of the valley by Staple Edge Wood. These two quarries are highly favoured economically because the steeply-dipping strata facilitate extraction of the rock and both are close to the main road. Nearby can be seen some old shafts of two famous iron mines, Buckshaft and Shakemantle, which produced nearly two million tons of iron ore between 1841 and 1899. The vast heaps of cinders from older iron works may have given rise to the name of Cinderford, for iron working was carried on in Dean at least two thousand years ago.

The Cinderford Brook which flows past Ruspidge to Soudley has carved out a very deep, ravine-like valley, resembling a miniature Wye gorge, with thick forests on either side leading southwards to Blakeney, the area dealt with in the next chapter.

Chapter 6

The Blakeney-Soudley Area

SMALL towns and villages have grown up along the main road from Gloucester to Chepstow at places where roads lead off northwards into the Forest of Dean. Most of these roads follow deep valleys for, in general, from Lydney to Newnham the drainage pattern is north-south. Down these valleys came iron ore and oak logs for the navy in Tudor times. Blakeney is located where two valleys drained by the Blackpool and Soudley brooks provide natural routeways into Dean. The area just north of Blakeney offers some of the finest scenery in the Forest, yet it is not much frequented as it is off the main tracks to the tourist centres of Symond's Yat and Tintern Abbey. In this area the archaeologist and historian can find many interesting features, including an exposed section of the Roman road at Blackpool Bridge, the Elizabethan associations at Gatcombe and the old Severn railway bridge at Purton.

Viney and Blakeney hills seem to dominate the village of Blakeney for they command the entrances to the two valleys leading to Cinderford and Parkend. The sketch, Figure 29, shows that Blakeney Hill with its southerly aspect, overlooking the town and yet within a stone's throw of the Forest, is highly

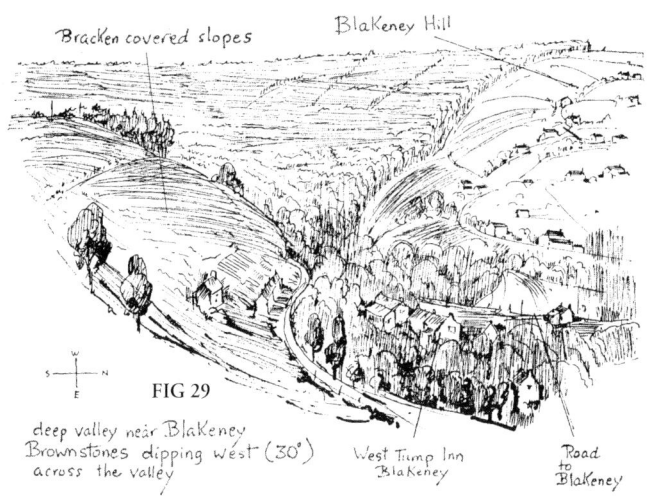

FIG 29

Bracken covered slopes
Blakeney Hill
deep valley near Blakeney
Brownstones dipping west (30°) across the valley
West Tump Inn Blakeney
Road to Blakeney

Geology Explained in the Forest of Dean and Wye Valley

favoured for settlement. The sketch also shows how the great depth of the valley seems almost to force the bijou bungalows and cosy cottage dwellings to climb up the hillside.

This chapter will be mainly concerned with the Devonian rocks, the Brownstones and the St Maughan's group. The plan is to proceed northwards to Blackpool Bridge and Soudley and then to return to Blakeney by the Soudley Brook valley.

A general view of Viney Hill, Figure 30, shows part of the southern rim of the Forest of Dean which is still high but does not present such a wall-like barrier as that on the eastern side on account of the north-south valleys which allow easy entry. Rivers usually erode their valleys in softer rocks or along the strike – a line of direction at right-angles to the dip as explained in the inset diagram in Figure 30. Both valleys at Blakeney are almost strike valleys, although not many rivers in the Forest of Dean are adjusted to rock structures, as will be seen in the chapters on The Wye valley.

The impressive depth of the valley is indicated in Figure 29 of Blakeney Hill. A pause should be made by the West Tump Inn, for on the other side of the road there is an old railway cutting which reveals the true nature of the Brownstones in this region (Figure 31). The sandstones dip across the valley at an angle of 20 degrees and as the old railway line, built to carry coal, followed the valley, problems arose in the various cuttings. The

FIG 30

Viney Hill 500 ft

River Severn old railway bridge

Viney Hill

many old quarries in sandstones of the Brownstones group dip 25° West

FIG 31

old railway cutting near
Tump House, Blakeney.
massive sandstones —
— Brownstones, dip 20° West

sandstones led to slip down on the track and masonry was necessary to wall up the cuttings. Civil engineers have encountered similar problems in the construction of the motorway which is being built through the steeply dipping Brownstones between Ross-on-Wye and Monmouth. The micaceous nature of these sandstones, together with the interbedded shales, make them split easily into flagstones and this natural gift to builders was first used by the Romans, as can be seen in the visible portion of the Roman road by Blackpool Bridge. Towards Blackpool Bridge, the almost gorge-like winding valley is thickly forested but in places where trees have been cut down more open country gives way to bracken covered, steep slopes where the geology can be examined without resorting to quarries. This is the Danby Lodge area and the red sandy soils on the forest roads along the lower slopes indicate the underlying Devonian rocks, whilst higher up very light, buff-coloured sandy soils show the presence of the Coal Measures. The Danby Lodge

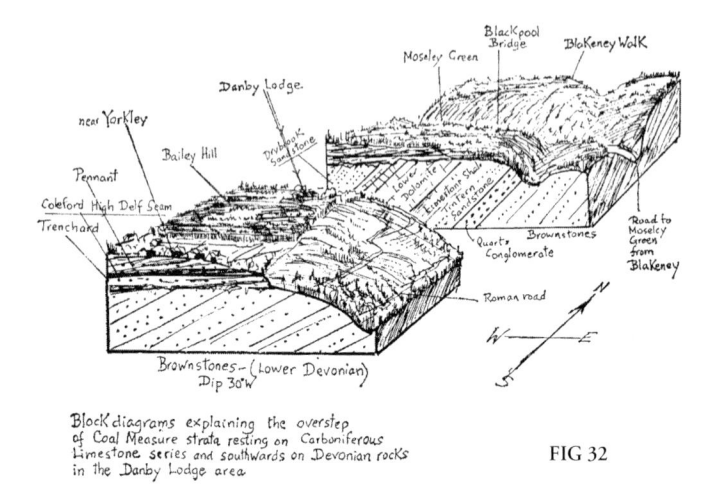

Block diagrams explaining the overstep of Coal Measure strata resting on Carboniferous Limestone series and southwards on Devonian rocks in the Danby Lodge area

FIG 32

area is thus an important one in the Forest for from here across to Lydney the Coal Measures overstep from the Carboniferous Limestone series onto the Devonian. This very clear example of unconformity is explained in two block diagrams, Figure 32.

A few hours should be spent in this important area and there are plenty of forest tracks for walkers, as well as parking spaces on the verge. The best section in the whole of the Forest of Dean for showing the unconformity is in a large old quarry near Moseley Green (Figure 33). Here the massive Lower Dolomite dips at a very steep angle, 70 degrees to the west, and on the cliff top can be seen thinly-bedded Coal Measure sandstones and shales resting at a different angle of dip on the upturned edges of the Lower Dolomite. The writer has been successful in persuading the Forestry Commission to preserve this fine example, as such well-exposed unconformities are 'classic' scenes for the geologist.

Now we can follow the Roman road southwards from Blackpool Bridge and climb up to Danby Lodge. Here the visitor will be able to do his geology without visiting quarries for the block diagram shows how the topography conforms to the general arrangement of the strata. Walking along the top forestry road one is almost following the junction of the Coal Measures and the upturned edges of the Brownstones. In 1967 a man from Yorkley was working a 'one man mine' on the edge of the Forest here, and the pit heap of blue-grey shale is an easily recognised sign of the workings. As one looks northwards from Danby Lodge, not a town or village can be seen for vast pine forests stretching to the horizon cover both Devonian and Carboniferous rocks. Generally speaking, conifers thrive as well on the sandstones of the Coal Measures as on those of the Devonian. The most economic use of sandy tracts of country is, therefore, to plant conifers, especially the quick-growing larch trees.

The minor road from Blackpool Bridge to Soudley passes the Drummer Boy Stone, a block of Devonian Conglomerate with an artificial hollow containing some smelted iron ore. Its origin is unknown but the stone must have come from the outcrop of the Quartz Conglomerate only a few hundred yards away. Farther north in the Soudley area, we find quite a labyrinth of valleys all deep in the Forest, but we now turn to go south by the Soudley Brook valley back to Blakeney. Soudley Pond (Figure

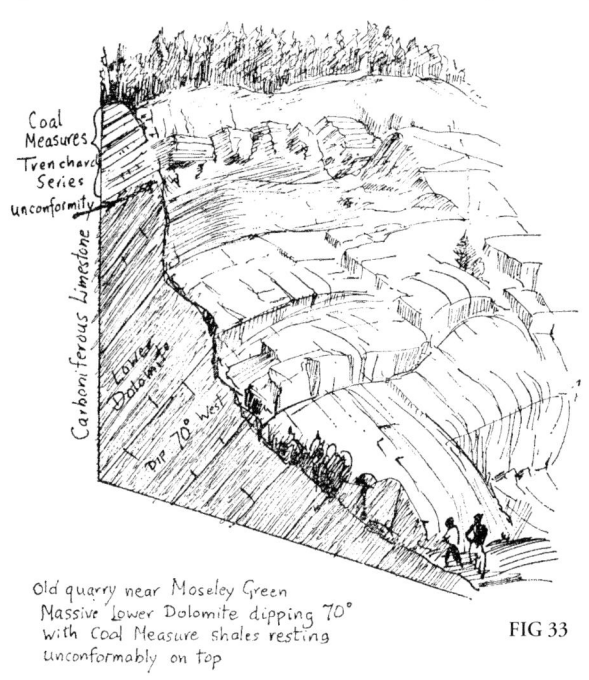

FIG 33

Old quarry near Moseley Green
Massive lower Dolomite dipping 70°
with Coal Measure shales resting
unconformably on top

Soudley Pond near Soudley

FIG 34

34) is a relic of the days when iron foundries were very active in this area for it provided power for the forges.

The Soudley valley is deeper than the one by which we came up to Blackpool, too deep, in fact, for the road to follow the valley floor as it winds its way to Two Bridges. Here, one side of the valley is much lower than the other because there are softer rocks outcropping on the eastern side. The block diagram, Figure 35, shows how the Brownstones strike across the valley at Two Bridges with the series known as the St Maughan's group outcropping on the eastern side. These rocks are of Lower Devonian age and, being composed of soft marls, give rise to a more subdued type of relief. The Electricity Board had some difficulty in taking cables across this deep valley, and local residents declare that the span between the pylons here is the longest in the country. It will be noticed that, as in the case of the other parallel valley, it becomes deeper to the south, the reason for which will be explained in a later chapter on the origin of the Wye gorge.

A pleasant afternoon can be spent examining the nature of the St Maughan's group of Lower Devonian rocks which outcrop on the cliffs at Gatcombe. Here they consist of red marls with green streaks and occasional bands of calcareous nodules, a much softer rock than the Brownstones, and we shall see in the Lydney area how the St Maughan's group can be distinguished by the lower relief. Further downstream at Purton are cliffs in the same rocks but access to the foreshore by the old Severn railway bridge is difficult and rubber boots should be worn by anyone wishing to examine these cliffs. The massive stone pillars of the bridge (now being dismantled) have lasted well since its construction in 1874, but unfortunately some ten years ago part of the bridge was broken by a barge which became lost in the fog while the pilot was trying to find the entrance to the Berkeley Canal at Sharpness.

This short chapter is concluded by again emphasising the importance of the Danby Lodge area in demonstrating the chief structural features that have shaped the Forest of Dean.

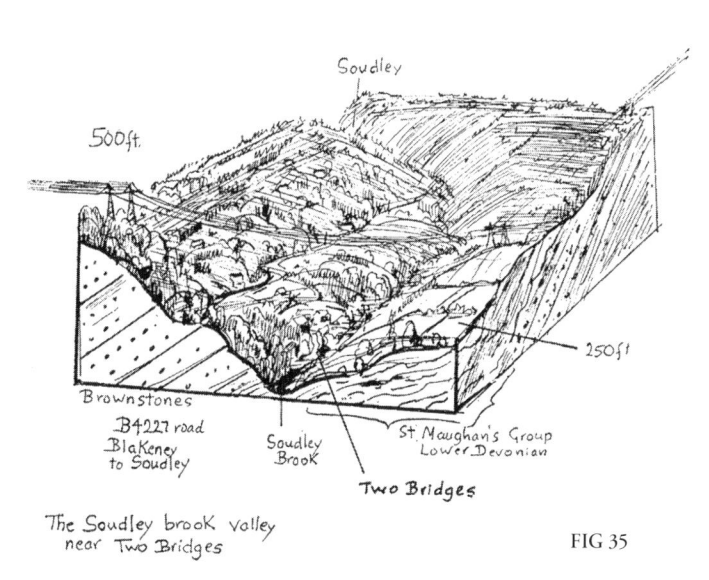

The Soudley brook valley near Two Bridges

FIG 35

Chapter 7
Lydney Area and Beachley-Clanna Pericline

THE area dealt with in this chapter is on the south-western side of Dean and extends from Lydney to Tidenham. The limits of his region are easily defined because it is a structural unit known as the Beachley-Clanna pericline. The structure is an anticline or dome with its main axis stretching from Priors Mesne to near Woolaston, giving a rather oval shape; the term pericline is used for such a structure. It is matched by the Lydney syncline on the east and the Tidenham syncline on the west, all part of the Hercynian and earlier folding mentioned in Chapter 3. A very prolonged period of erosion followed the uplift, in which many thousands of feet of sediment were removed so that today the core is exposed with the oldest rocks in the centre. This is really a miniature weald similar to the Sussex Weald where an eroded dome, with the oldest rocks in the centre, is almost encircled by younger rocks, the chalk hills of the North and South Downs.

The geological sketch map, Figure 36, shows that about half the structure is visible and it is safe to assume that the southern portion extends under the bed of the Severn. The small arrows on the map which show the dip of the strata indicate that the anticlinal structure is asymmetrical, the steepest limb of the fold being on the west, a common feature of the Dean folds. (See Figure 9 in Chapter 3.) The block diagram Figure 37, shows how the nearly parallel scarps are caused by the inclined strata, the major one being formed by the Quartz Conglomerate, which once again turns up as a main physical feature. The second scarp is the Lower dolomite of the Carboniferous Limestone series which presents a bold feature in the Tidenham area. The block diagram shows that the encircling forested scarps hem in the region, maintaining the isolation of the central portion and, once inside, the visitor finds that exits to the north, west and east are steep and difficult. Although the main A48 Gloucester to Chepstow road makes a traverse of the structural unit, the visitor who turns off to investigate finds himself in a veritable cul-de-sac.

Lydney is a kind of foothill town at one of the major gateways to the Forest of Dean, created by one of the typical deep valleys such as those at Blakeney. The tributaries that drain the Forest of Dean plateau have certain features in common; they rise on the plateau

The Lydney Area and Beachley-Clanna Pericline

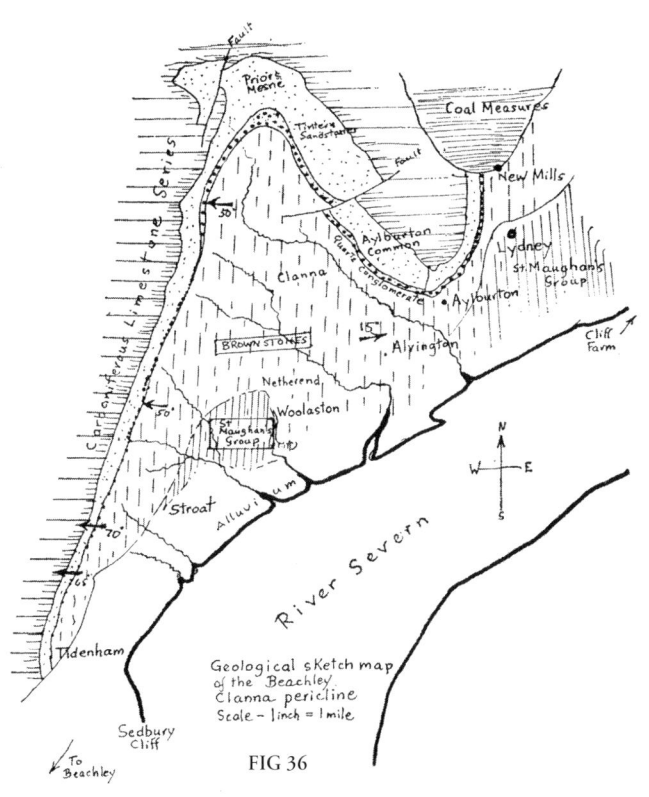

FIG 36 — Geological sketch map of the Beachley Clanna pericline. Scale – 1 inch = 1 mile

as tiny streams in open, wide valleys but, on nearing the plateau edge, the gradient increases rapidly and the streams become entrenched in steep-sided gorges before entering either the Wye valley or the plains bordering the Severn estuary. This is well seen if we proceed northwards from Lydney to New Mills where we follow the Cannop Brook, one of the major north-south valleys in Dean. At New Mills, the steep valley sides are in the Devonian rocks (Brownstones), but just at this point the unconformity where the Coal Measures overstep the Devonian can be easily seen in a forestry road above the old Norchard Colliery. There are many fine forest walks in this area and in both Norchard Wood and around Primrose Hill the junction of the Lower Devonian red rocks with the yellow-brown sandstones of the Coal Measures (Trenchard series) can be seen. The construction of forest roads has done much to help the geologist for there are numerous cuttings exposing the various strata. At Ten Acre Wood, north of Primrose Hill, a small coal seam is visible on a forest roadside cutting. These cuttings are soon overgrown and the writer has asked the Forestry Commission to preserve such sites, for it is far better to see a seam of coal in the open than to delve down a mine with a carbide lamp. Following the B4231 road from Lydney to Bream, we observe that the beginning of the Coal Measures almost coincides with the entry of the road into the forest just north of Blackrock Farm.

Permission to enter Lydney Park must be obtained from the estate office. The scenery is picturesque with steep hills formed of the Lower Dolomite and the deep gorge of the Park Brook, which is close to the Roman temple. Sir Mortimer Wheeler, who worked on this archaeological site, declared that the iron mine ear the villa was the only example in Britain to provide direct evidence that the Romans mined iron ore in Dean. If this valley is followed northwards for a mile, the most famous 'scowles' area in Dean will be seen, and it is significant that the Quartz Conglomerate crops out in the Park over low-lying ground without he scarp feature that might be expected. Briefly, it could be explained that the rim of the Dean saucer is not everywhere level and in places is depressed to low levels, so that wherever it is tilted up a bold scarp is formed.

The main road from Lydney to Chepstow cuts right across the Beachley-Clanna pericline, so that

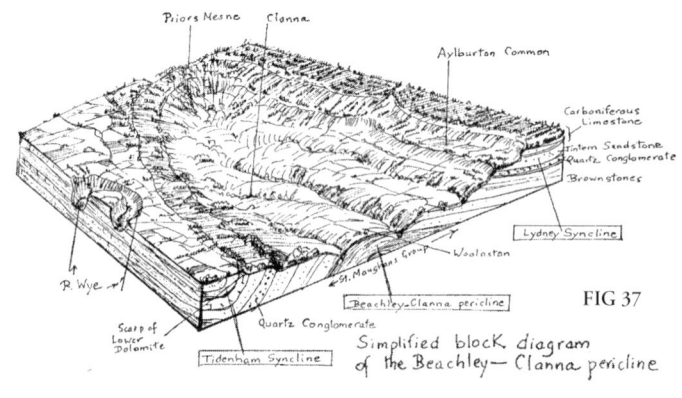

FIG 37

Simplified block diagram of the Beachley—Clanna pericline

The Lydney Area and Beachley-Clanna Pericline

FIG 38 — Priors Mesne at the northern rim of the Beachley-Clanna Pericline. (Labels: scarp of Lower Dolomite; scarp of Quartz Conglomerate)

on most parts of the road one can see the whole structure as depicted in the block diagram, Figure 37. A good point of entry is at the village of Aylburton, where a by-road leads to Aylburton Common. Here the Quartz Conglomerate dips eastwards at 15 degrees resulting in a much wider outcrop than is given by the more usual steeper dip of 30 degrees: the rough ground created by the hard pudding stone gives Aylburton an extensive common from which one can enjoy wonderful views of the Severn bridge and the Severn estuary. Viewed from the hills above Tidenham on the other side of the anticline, this glorious common presents a shelf-like relief feature shown on the block diagram. One can explore the heart of this miniature 'weald' by numerous by-ways and footpaths which, in places, resemble the leafy lanes of Sussex in pre-war days. One of these leads to Priors Mesne (Figure 38), tucked away in a sheltered corner of the 'weald' and nestling under the bold craggy scarp of the Quartz Conglomerate. The Cone Brook has cut right through the densely wooded scarps near Clanna Woods but it flows through a deep, ravine-like valley that no road follows it, though it is possible for the adventurous to trace its course on foot to Cone Pill on the Severn estuary. This stream once provided power for a series of mills, and along its course one can still see evidence of a former grain mill at Rodmore, a cardboard mill

FIG 39 Dolomitic Conglomerate - TRIAS

fossil plain or erosion platform

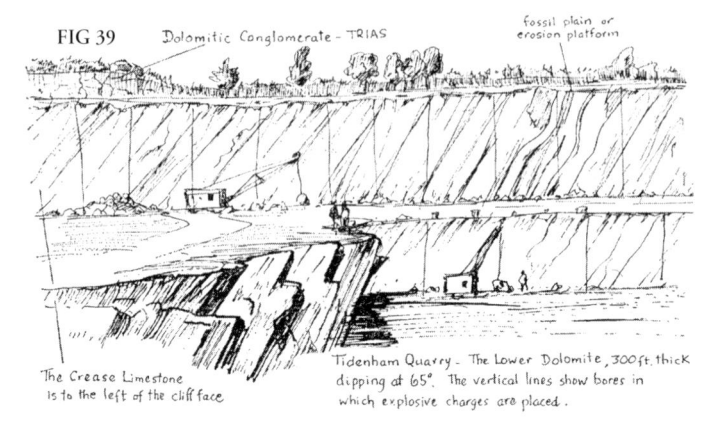

The Crease Limestone is to the left of the cliff face

Tidenham Quarry - The Lower Dolomite, 300ft thick dipping at 65°. The vertical lines show bores in which explosive charges are placed.

at Rowley, a paper mill at Cone and another grain mill lower down towards the pill, all within a distance of about two miles.

Continuing into the core of the dome, by way of Woolaston, we find that the ground is higher and more undulating on the Brownstone series of the Lower Devonian at about 300 feet than on the outcrop of the softer rocks in the St Maughan's group. The altitude between Stroat and Woolaston averages only 150 feet and the farmland here is good because of the calcareous soils derived from this group. Sandstone is a very permeable rock and will hold considerable quantities of water locked up in the pore spaces between the tiny grains of sand, and as the core of the anticline is largely made up of this type of rock it is not surprising that there are numerous springs all around the foot of the major scarp of the Clay Hill, half a mile east of Hewelsfield, where the open field country on the Carboniferous Limestones contrasts with the thickly forested scarps bordering the region.

At Tidenham, on the main road to Chepstow from Gloucester, is the entrance to a very busy quarry in the Lower Dolomite which helps to supply increased demands by the Ministry of Transport for hard road aggregate in the construction of motorways. Some of the dolomite is sent to the steel works in South Wales for use as a flux in the blast furnaces. The sketch, Figure 39, shows that the Lower Dolomite has a very steep dip of 65 degrees. In order to extract the rock for crushing, vertical drills are made at intervals and filled with explosive to blast out the rock. However, the most remarkable feature here is the horizontal surface across the upturned strata. The top of the cliff looks as though it had been sliced off with a knife; it is in fact an ancient or fossil plain which geomorphologists term 'an erosion platform'. In this quarry one is looking at an ancient plain eroded during the period of Triassic deserts some 200 million years ago. As evidence of this, patches of the debris can be seen on the top left (shown in Figure 39), forming a deposit known as the Dolomitic Conglomerate. This is really a consolidated scree of waste rock from the limestone hills bordering the Triassic desert plains. (Some doubt could be raised by a suggestion that this plain was formed in a later geological period.) If we climb to the cliff top we can see that it is made of angular fragments of the Carboniferous Limestones of the same type as on the quarry face, and set in a red marl matrix. This is the base of the Trias and the quarry workers are now uncovering a fossil landscape surface. Residual patches of this Dolomitic breccia (a breccia contains angular pieces of rock whereas in a conglomerate the pieces are rounded or pebbly), which occur in many places in the Chepstow area and on the other side of the Severn, help the geologist to reconstruct the ancient landscapes way back in geological time. Elsewhere, the base of the Trias is a conglomerate.

A complete change of scene is afforded by three beaches with cliffs which, because of their greater extent, are far better than quarries for studying geology. At Cliff Farm, about a mile up river from Lydney, one can descend to a beach from the cliff top by the 'Jacob's Ladder' steps well known for salmon putchers. Here we can see cliffs of the St Maughan's group of the Lower Devonian, which are red marls with limestone concretions. Mention

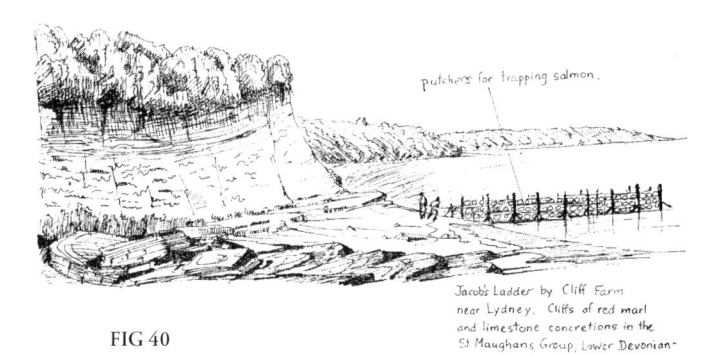

FIG 40

Jacob's Ladder by Cliff Farm near Lydney. Cliffs of red marl and limestone concretions in the St Maughans Group, Lower Devonian.

has already been made of the soft nature of these rocks in other areas and how they give rise to low relief yet good farmland. Figure 40 shows that there are underlying strata of steeply-inclined sandstones forming a natural protection to the foreshore. It is interesting to make a collection of the various pebbles which have been brought down by the Severn from the Midlands in recent times and deposited on the beach. Pebbles of white quartz (vein quartz), flint and Bunter Sandstone all have a history. The flints could have been brought from Lincolnshire chalk country by rivers from the melting ice sheets some 20,000 years ago, while the dark, slate-like pebbles might have originated from North Wales. This is a good place to take children for practical studies as small caves formed by tidal scours can be explored, and various rock formations can be observed and explained.

Sedbury Cliff is reached by taking a branch road from Tutshill and then following Offa's Dyke, which leads to the beginning of the cliffs. The main cliff face is of the Keuper Marl (Trias) but these rocks give way to the black shales of the Rhaetic near the top and above this are the thin bands of limestone of the Lower Lias (Jurassic) forming the flat-topped surface of the cliffs. The foreshore is strewn with blocks of both Rhaetic and Liassic rocks which are very fossiliferous, the latter being particularly prolific in the bivalve, *Ostrea liassica,* and various types of ammonites. Sedbury Cliff is, in fact, the best hunting ground in the whole of the Wye and Dean region for fossil collectors, the finest specimens, especially ammonites, being found further north around

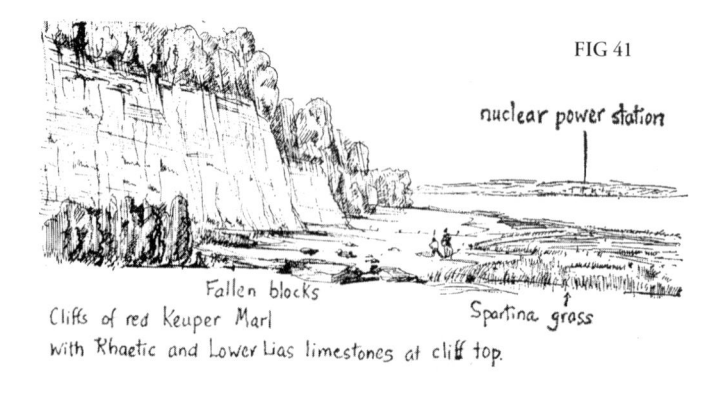

FIG 41

Cliffs of red Keuper Marl with Rhaetic and Lower Lias limestones at cliff top. Fallen blocks. Spartina grass. nuclear power station

FIG 42

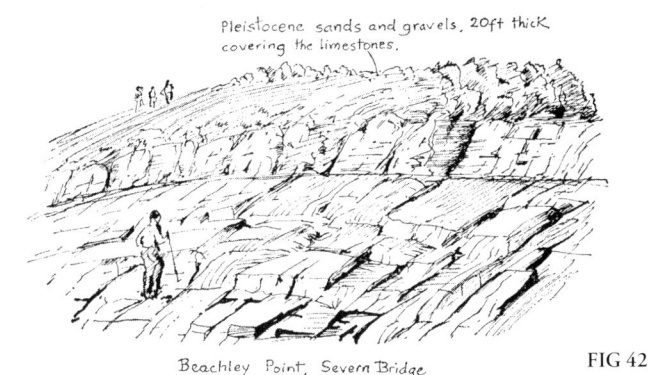

Beachley Point, Severn Bridge.
A small anticline structure in the Carboniferous Limestone just above high tide level. In some of the fissures are masses of the Dolomitic Conglomerate, the base of the Trias, in this locality

Pleistocene sands and gravels, 20ft thick covering the limestones.

the headland. Surface water percolating through the limestones above is released at the junction with the shales and, being rich in dissolved calcium bicarbonate, redeposits this as calcium carbonate in many calcareous springs lower down the cliff face. This deposit, known as 'tufa', consists of petrified moss, grass, twigs and wood, and large masses of this tumble down to the foreshore. The underlying wet shales form a lubricated surface on which masses of the Rhaetic and Lower Lias rocks tumble down and the sketch, Figure 41, shows a cliff mass that has slipped down. Masses of slipped clay make the trip quite a boggy one in places, yet it is interesting because here in high summer are found very large horsetails, *Equisetum*, 3 to 4 feet in height, whose ancestors were the giant trees known as 'Calamites' which flourished in the Coal Measure swamps 280 million years ago. The tidal mud flats are being colonised by the hybrid grass plant, *Spartina townsendi*, a good example of plant evolution which, in the last fifty years, has colonised many tidal mud flats around the coasts of Britain with an entirely new species. There is a deep natural channel here, so that boats making for the entrance to the Berkeley canal at Sharpness come close to the cliffs and the stillness is sometimes broken by the thump of marine engines or the noise of loudspeakers in the nuclear power station at Oldbury on the opposite shore.

A great contrast to the beaches at Sedbury and Cliff Farm is that at

Beachley where the hard limestones of the Carboniferous series crop out on the foreshore. These hard rocks form the basement on which the towers of the great Severn bridge have been built, and without these rocks there could have been no bridge here. Figure 42 shows that the limestones are thrown into folds (anticlines and synclines) which continue across the bed of the river forming islands and reefs in places. One of the towers of the bridge can also be seen to rest on one such small island. The limestones are partly dolomitic and well fissured, some of the gaping joints being filled with patches of the Dolomitic Conglomerate. A number of Carboniferous corals can be seen on the rock surfaces and a small fault near the headland has brought the limestones up against a cliff of the Keuper Marl. Beachley Point is a peninsula of limestone 'basement', but the flat-topped cliffs are covered with sands and gravels to a depth of twenty-three feet. These deposits are of Pleistocene age, and were probably related to interglacial periods when the Severn flowed at higher levels. Both Beachley and Sedbury cliffs are much less frequented now than in the days of the Aust ferry service, when travellers using the ferry had to pass near them. Access to the Severn bridge is from the other side of the Wye and the motorist now looks down on these cliffs from the heights of the motorway over the river.

Chapter 8

Hope Mansel Dome and Wigpool Syncline

THIS area is similar to the Clanna pericline and, though smaller, is also a dome structure measuring only two miles across. It stretches from Puddlebrook in the south to Pontshill in the north and from Wigpool in the east to Hope Mansel in the west. Like the Clanna area, it is almost a cul-de-sac with no central village, Hope Mansel itself being marginal and just a tiny hamlet. The Wigpool promontory plateau is included in this area.

The structure is a dome which was folded during the intra-Carboniferous period of earth movements, the folding affecting the Devonian and Lower Carboniferous rocks but not the Coal Measures. The geological map below, shows that the outcrops of strata are U-shaped and there is the usual scarp formed by the Quartz Conglomerate which not only rims the area but borders the complementary syncline of Wigpool. The corresponding syncline on the west is centred at Howle Hill but lies a few miles off our region and is not included in this chapter. The map shows that the Brownstones of the Lower Devonian occupy the sore of the anticline and the dips from 30 to 40 degrees tend to be steeper on the western side. The Coal

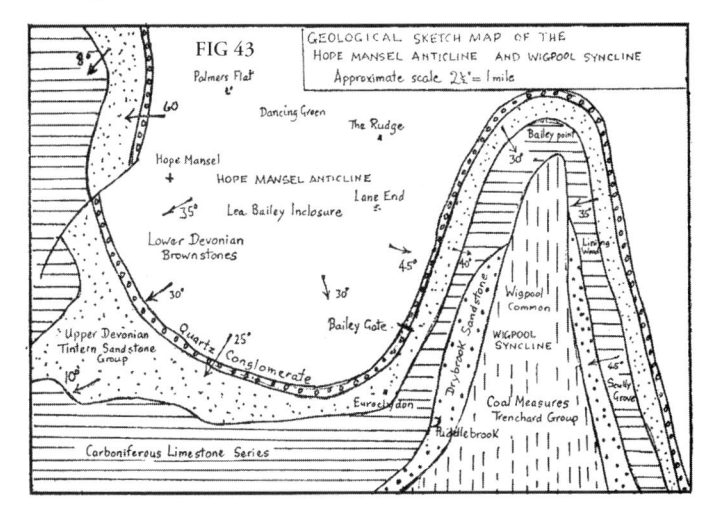

FIG 43 — GEOLOGICAL SKETCH MAP OF THE HOPE MANSEL ANTICLINE AND WIGPOOL SYNCLINE. Approximate scale 2½" = 1 mile

Measures overstep some of the Carboniferous Limestone series in the Wigpool region but do not rest on the Devonian, as in the Lydney area. The block diagram, Figure 44, has been adapted from G. H. Dury's book, *The Face of the Earth* (Pelican Books), this well-known author having chosen the Hope Mansel dome as an example of the correlation between patterns of drainage and structure. Here at Bailey Point at the end of the Wigpool promontory the entire landscape of the eroded dome can be observed in one view. Teachers of geography could use this view for comparisons with the Wealden region of south-eastern England.

The diagrams in Figure 45 show the development of scarps as a dome is eroded, but it has been very much simplified; for example, in stage one, all the succeeding strata of the Drybrook Sandstone, Coal Measures and even perhaps Mesozoic sediments would have covered this dome. In the course of millions of years an enormous mass of sediment has been removed by erosion, thicknesses of the order of several thousands of feet having all been carried away by the simple agents of weathering and running water. It is an understanding of these processes that helps the student who is beginning geology to appreciate the geological concept of time.

The entrance to the region is best made at Puddlebrook, where a visit should be made to the nearby quarry in the Drybrook Sandstone which reaches a maximum thickness of 350 feet in the Wigpool syncline. Boulders of this rock can be seen

BLOCK DIAGRAM OF THE HOPE MANSEL DOME AND WIGPOOL SYNCLINE

FIG 44

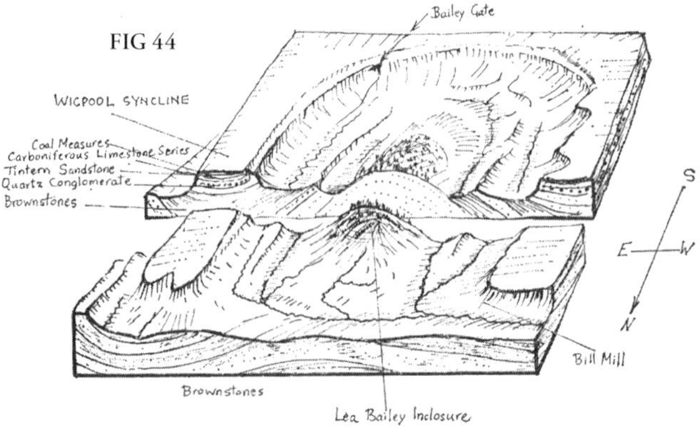

The Hope Mansel Dome and Wigpool Syncline

Stage 1 formation of intra-Carboniferous Fold

Dome or anticline, Lower Carboniferous, Devonian

Stage 2 erosion of fold

Coal Measure Swamp forests

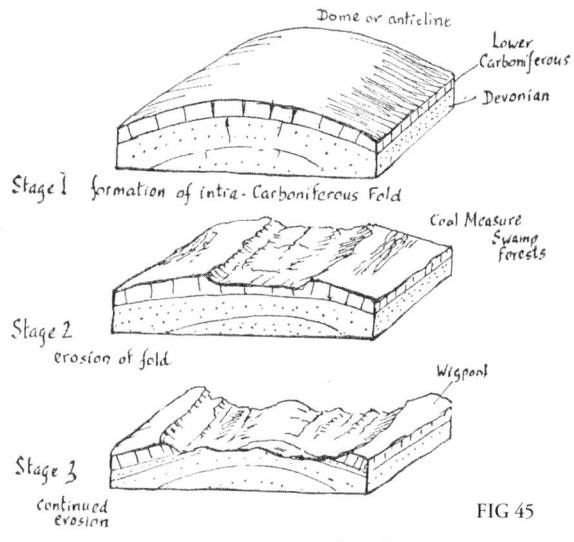

Stage 3 continued erosion

Wigpool

FIG 45

Diagrams showing the formation of scarps from an eroded anticline.

some fifteen feet below the cliff top which is perhaps part of the unconformity so well shown in the old railway cutting at Drybrook, an excellent section now almost obscured by vegetation and rubbish. Near to the Euroclydon Hotel, and on the roadside leading northwards from Drybrook to Weston-under-Penyard, is an important section which shows the junction of the Upper Devonian Tintern Sandstone with the lowest division of the Carboniferous Limestone series, the Lower Limestone Shale. Here the Tintern Sandstone is about 300 feet thick and the cliffs abut on to rather a busy road, making it difficult for even the careful observer to note the change to a sandy crinoidal limestone which indicates the sea advancing over the Devonian lands at the beginning of the Carboniferous period some 350 million years ago.

Lower down but still on the roadside, at Bailey Gate, there is a very good exposure of the Quartz Conglomerate which is here about 100 feet thick and consists of two distinct bands of the 'pudding stone' separated by bands of pebbly sandstone (Figure 46). The rock is strongly jointed so that masses become detached and tumble downhill, sometimes on to the road. The geologist can easily study the core of this dome as there are numerous forestry roads in the Lea Bailey Inclosure where one can see the Brownstones in small cuttings. They consist of either massive sandstones or flaggy sandstones with interbedded soft marls and purply grey shales. It is from these many small exposures that the various dips can be mapped and thus prove the anticlinal structure of the entire region. The small scarps of the valleys within the dome area are formed of more massive sandstones, the best example being the ridge bearing the road along to The Rudge (Figure 47). Seen from a distance, the view reveals how the drainage pattern, the field boundaries, topography and even human settlement are all controlled by the geological structure and lithology. One must remember that the major part of this dome is formed of a great thickness of sandstones which provide natural storage for water. One inch of rainfall equals 101 tons of water per acre, and as the annual rainfall of this area of some 3,000 acres is about 30 inches one can imagine that after many thousands of years a tremendous amount of water must have accumulated in spite of normal drainage downwards. There are many springs which have given rise to small settlements, eg Dancing Green, Lane End, Palmer's Flat and Hope Mansel, and even today many cottagers get their water supply from local wells.

FIG 46
Bailey Gate. Outcrop of the Quartz Conglomerate

The Hope Mansel Dome and Wigpool Syncline

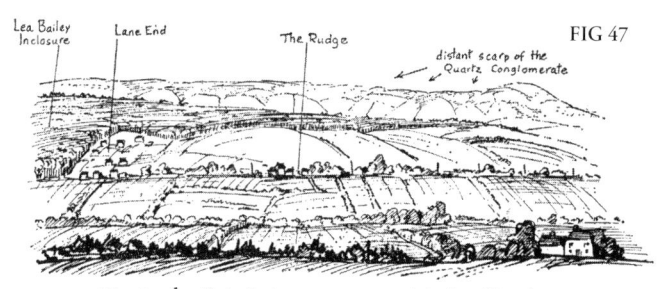

The view from Bailey Point across the core of the Hope Mansel Dome. **FIG 47**

For those who are prepared to rough it and undertake some rock climbing, there are quite precipitous cliffs of the Quartz Conglomerate exposed in Knackers Hole Grove just above Bill Mill (Figure 48). Reference to the geological map shows a fault on the western side of the dome near Hope Mansel, and the effect of this is to throw the scarp of the Quartz Conglomerate forward on the downthrow side of the fault. Diagrams in Figure 49 explain this situation and Figure 50 shows the distant scarp crowned with forest. It can also be seen how the forest boundary changes with the fault, a good example of vegetation revealing the geological structure.

The Wigpool syncline area extends from Bailey Point to Puddlebrook, an oval-shaped promontory jutting out like a headland into the

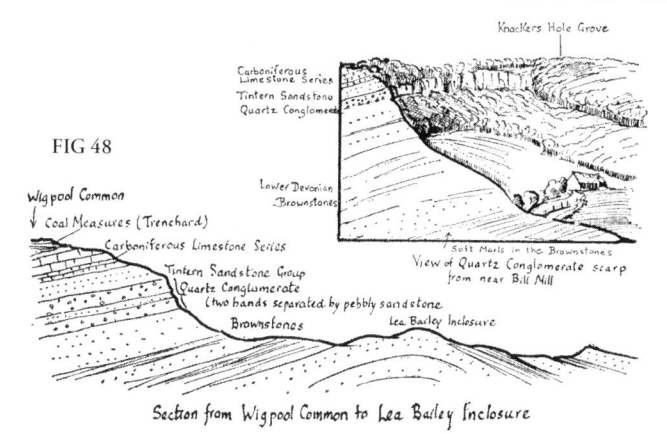

FIG 48

Section from Wigpool Common to Lea Bailey Inclosure

northern plains. Although rather a featureless forested plateau, 800 to 900 feet high, it gives splendid views of other parts of Dean. Eastwards, the view is dominated by the great dome-shaped mass of May Hill, an inlier of Silurian rocks and a continuation of the Malvern axis. Westwards, the panorama which lies before us is shown in Figure 51. The Trenchard series of the Coal Measures, consisting mainly of sandstones with basal conglomerates, covers most of the plateau to a thickness of some 300 feet. The sandy soils are largely given over to extensive conifer plantations which make this promontory quite a landmark in Dean. There is not much evidence of former coal mining, and coal seams of economic value are absent. One indication of this is the presence of what are termed 'red beds' in the Coal Measures here. These consist of reddish shales and mudstones and may indicate arid conditions with sparse vegetation at the time of deposition, whereas in other areas in Dean there were vast swamp forests which later produced the seams of coal.

In the centre of the plateau is the shaft of the Wigpool Iron Mine which ceased to operate in 1918. The shaft was sunk through 300 feet of Coal Measure sandstones and 200 feet of Drybrook Sandstone before reaching pockets of iron ore in the Crease Limestone at a depth of 530 feet. Although most of the iron ore came from the Crease Limestone some was also found in the Lower Dolomite, and the underground workings under Wigpool Common are said to be quite extensive. There are many entrances to underground workings in a 'scowles' area between Lining Wood and Wigpool Common. The bizarre shapes of these ancient workings for iron ore may be well seen in the Devil's Chapel on the other side of the Forest of Dean at Bream. Similar 'scowles' can be seen on the eastern side of Wigpool Common where the outcrop of the Carboniferous Limestones occurs. One such 'scowle', known locally as 'The Yankee Cinema', was used during

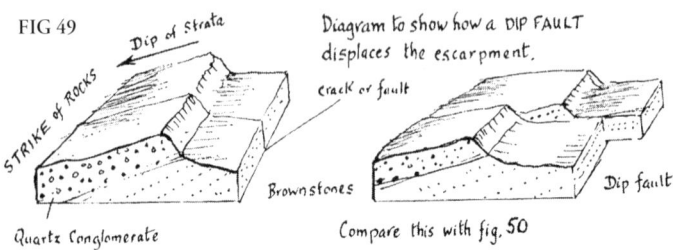

FIG 49

Diagram to show how a DIP FAULT displaces the escarpment.

Compare this with fig. 50

The Hope Mansel Dome and Wigpool Syncline

Hope Mansel — fault in the scarp revealed by shift of position. the wooded scarp the Quartz Conglomerate — *Lea Bailey Inclosure*

FIG 50

The Hope Mansel Dome. In the foreground is the Lea Bailey Inclosure which is the core of the anticline.

the war as an open-air cinema by American troops stationed nearby. Little did the old miners know that their underground delvings would later provide a natural stage and auditorium for foreign soldiers.

At the extreme northern tip of the Wigpool promontory, Bailey Point, there is a good cliff face of the Lower Dolomite and if we follow the margin of the plateau around on both eastern and western sides we find numerous small quarries in the Carboniferous Limestones, many of which are so overgrown that access is very difficult. All over the country many well-known quarries have become thickly colonised with vegetation very soon after being abandoned. Even the local people complain about this state of affairs since quarries form natural playgrounds for village children.

Country folk declare that in the old days rabbits kept the quarries much to the farmers' disgust, geologists would be pleased to see the rabbits back! One of the few good quarries still accessible is in Scully Grove about half a mile west of Mitcheldean, where a cliff face shows the upper part to be of the Drybrook Sandstone and the lower part of the Carboniferous Limestone series termed the Whitehead Limestone, an interesting feature here being the algal type of limestone. Some limestones are formed of microscopic calcareous algae, their remains forming minute concentric structures, but here there are 'giant' specimens, three-quarters of an inch in size, and of types known as *Garwoodia* and *Mitcheldeania*.

Scattered about the plateau are many old cottages which were

Figure 51: View across the western limb of the Hope Mansel Dome from Parkfield House near Bill Mill. Labels: Euroclydon, Lea Bailey Enclosure, Hope Mansel, Purlieu Wood.

once inhabited by iron miners but in recent years have been sold to 'foreign invaders' seeking peace and seclusion, for here there is no bus service or shop and the only way out, except on foot, is to return by way of the Wigpool road to Mitcheldean or to Puddlebrook.

Old stories linger on in remote places such as this, and in many parts of the Forest of Dean former miners have told the writer about the gold mine here. As with most fairy tales, this story of about the gold mine here. As with most fairy tales, this story of a gold mine probably contains some grains of truth for when the Bailey Level was driven into the hill from the western side in order to drain out the water from the Wigpool Mine, the workings passed through the Quartz Conglomerate. As most mining engineers are aware, gold is often found as tiny specks in quartz and this may account for the story, although apparently no gold was found here. Because of the rock variations in a small area, the Wigpool syncline and Mansel dome are important 'field areas' for training geologists, and universities often send their students here to map the outcrops, and record dips and faults as part of their training for future work overseas. Indeed, the writer has met geologists in the outback of Australia who have done part of their field training in Dean.

From Wigpool, we look across to a detached part of the Forest at Dean plateau, Penyard Park and Chase Wood, a hill mass cut off, in all probability, due to erosion by the river Wye. The ancient river no longer flows here and the possible cause of its diversion is examined in the next chapter, the first of four in which we turn to the Wye valley, following a course from Ross past Monmouth and Tintern Abbey to Chepstow.

Chapter 9

The Wye Valley: Ross to Kerne Bridge

GEOLOGY is essentially a field science and much progress has been made in recent times by carefully recording the operation of natural processes such as river deposition and erosion, formation of deltas and sandbanks and the weathering of rocks in deserts, polar and tropical areas. In effect, it is a policy of first watching geology in the making under present-day conditions and this chapter will attempt to show how it can be applied while enjoying pleasant rambles along the Wye from Ross to Kerne Bridge.

On each side of this stretch of the river there is a footpath for the benefit of fishermen and canoeists, so there is plenty of scope for the rambler to wander in peace. It is, however, advisable to carry an Ordnance Survey map, preferably the 1:25,000 or 2½ inches to the mile scale, which shows all the footpaths and helps one to plan a day's trip. Without a map one can wander for many miles along the sweeping meanders of the Wye and finally arrive back very close to the starting point.

Close to Ross church, a footpath leads by way of the cricket ground across the meadows to the banks of the Wye in the area known as Tudorville. The banks of the river, about fifteen feet in height, show that in the recent past the river has deposited layers of chocolate-coloured silt which are well stratified. The colour leads one to suspect that the silt has originated from the erosion of Devonian rocks further upstream.

More detailed inspection of river cliffs shows that there are coarser layers interbedded with the clays and silts. This indicates that there were floods in which the river was able to carry down from the hills much coarser material, such as pebbles and even boulders, and if we find in the river gravels and silt some fragments of medieval pottery or bits of flint implements we can approximately date the age of the various layers. The important thing to note is that running water has sorted out the grains of minerals and rock according to size and deposited them in stratified layers under the influence of gravity. Occasionally we can see miniature folds developed where layers of unconsolidated sand have slid over masses of stratified silty clays, a feature referred as structures formed by slumping or sliding under gravity. Similar miniature folds, still beautifully preserved after 300 million years, are often found in Carboniferous mudstones in Dean, eg in Tintern Quarry, three miles

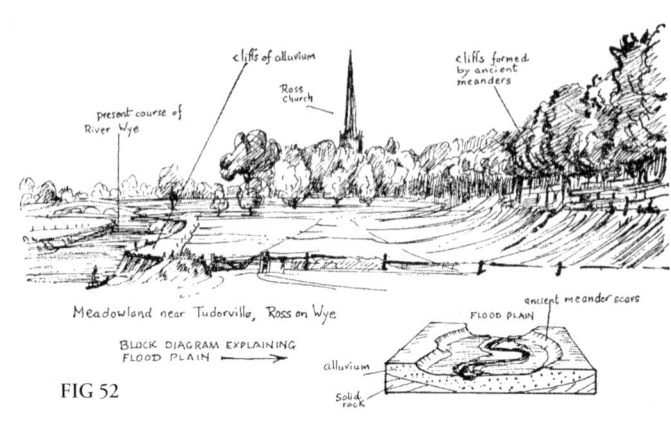

Geology Explained in the Forest of Dean and Wye Valley

FIG 52

Figure 52: Meadowland near Tudorville, Ross on Wye. Block diagram explaining flood plain.

north of Chepstow. Some cliffs may show thin layers of peat about ten feet from the top of the bank, which proves that vegetation has been buried under muds deposited by river floods.

The sketch, Figure 52, shows the meadowlands close to the old Wye bridge at Ross and the cliffs of sandstone, now about twenty feet above the present level of the river, which are quite natural, having been formed by the lateral erosion of river banks perhaps only a few hundred years ago. These meadowlands form what is known as the flood plain of the river and very often in winter all these fields may be under water for several weeks at a time. The inset diagram in Figure 52 shows that the river has a tendency to wander all over this flood plain unless the banks are stabilised by masonry or by the planting of such trees as willow, alder and poplar. The small cliffs shown are ancient meander scars which, if very well developed, form large river bluffs, and it is on such a bluff that the town of Ross has originated. In fact, many towns have been sited on river bluffs because a good bridging point could be established where an ancient meander scar or gravel terrace occurred close to the present course of the river. As in all rivers, the meanders of the Wye, with the exception of the gorge, are the outstanding feature. The puzzle is, why do rivers meander? Even today the answer is not definitely known. The diagrams in Figure 53 attempt to show what has been discovered by observing rivers under natural conditions. If a river is flowing on a fairly straight course, and this is rare, it will tend to develop deep pools and shallows at regular intervals.

Later, these become meanders which have a mathematical relationship, one wavelength being about ten times the width of the river when it is flowing high enough to reach the top of the bank. The amplitude of the meanders varies with the volume of water in the river and it can be observed that very regular meanders are developed when rivers flow through rocks that are all of the same texture and hardness, i.e. regular meanders will form in a homogeneous rock such as a clay or shale. In some cases a river meander may be cut off by erosion of the 'neck' as shown in Section C of Figure 53, for during the lateral erosion of rivers meanders tend to shift downstream; in fact, this is one of the ways in which a river builds up its own flood plain. If, however, a river comes up against an obstacle, whether it be a rock bar or a man-made feature such as a pier or dam, the meanders 'revolt' and behave in quite an irregular fashion before they settle down again. Section D of Figure 53 shows that if a climatic change occurs, eg a diminution in the annual rainfall, the river will develop 'mini-meanders' within he larger ones. All these features can be seen in a walk beside The river Wye from Ross to Kerne Bridge and in the Symond's Yat locality.

Before starting the riverside ramble, the cliffs by the roadside very close to the town centre of Ross must be examined. These cliffs, shown in Figure 54, have been exposed during road-making and quarrying. They consist of reddish sandstones of the Brownstone series in the Lower Devonian, and form one of the finest sections in the

FIG 53

A Mathematic relationship of regular meanders

B Irregular meanders due to natural and artificial obstacles

C Development of cut off lakes (ox bow lakes) by erosion of meander neck

D Present day "mini-meanders" developed on "fossil meanders, due to lower rainfall. (change of climate) and therefore less water flowing in the river".

MEANDERS

whole region which geologists can examine from the roadside with little effort.

Now we can start to apply what we know of the present to interpreting the past. In the sandstones, the bedding planes are fairly regularly spaced, indicating that deposition took place in comparatively regular cycles or rhythms, but in places the sandstone bands thin out and we can see layers of cross-bedding, as shown in Figure 55. These features show how river channels were cut out in older beds of silt and sand, while more vigorous erosion brought down pebbles and boulders which were all sorted out and stratified by the action of running water and gravity. Similar

FIG 54

Ross on Wye – Cliffs of Old Red Sandstone along the main road by the river

cross-bedding can be seen forming today in the semi-arid lands of the Middle East, where vast deposits are laid down on slopes after a spell of heavy thunderstorms.

Most of the pebbles in the sandstones are of vein quartz of the kind found in the Quartz Conglomerate, but some have dropped out of the surface layers leaving cavities. In places, there are larger cavities which were originally filled with nodules of marly clay. The action of water percolating through the solid rock has concentrated calcareous material at the junction of bedding planes, making them harder and leaving the intervening sandstones softer. This causes a peculiar feature known as honeycomb weathering in these cliffs, and it can also be seen in old castle walls or medieval buildings constructed of Old Red

Cross bedding in Old Red Sandstone cliffs, by the main road, Ross on Wye

honeycomb weathering

FIG 55

Sandstone where the blocks were cemented together by the builders. Streaks of a grey-green colour visible in many parts of the cliff section indicate a chemical change from the red ferric oxide of the sandstones to the reduced state of the ferrous oxide condition. This may be due either to organisms extracting some oxygen from the ferric oxide, or to a purely chemical change, known as a reducing condition, that occurred after consolidation of the rock. The reasons for the change are, however, not fully understood.

Thus, from these cliffs we can picture the desert conditions some 400 million years ago when the

Goodrich Castle from the River Wye

FIG 56

Goodrich Castle – Norman Keep built 1150 AD
The castle seems to grow up out of the Old Red Sandstones of which the castle is built. The deep, wide, rock-cut ditch is in the Brownstones (Lower Devonian) dipping at 30° East

FIG 57

plains were strewn with layers of gravel and sand brought down by torrents and where, during thunderstorm spells of heavy rain, the rivers cut out new channels. We see in these rocks no traces of plant or animal remains so we may surmise that it was indeed an arid landscape of widespread deltas, practically devoid of life. However, in the Wilderness Quarry in the Brownstones at Mitcheldean, remains of primitive fishes have been found embedded in the shales, evidence that the Devonian deserts had inland lakes like those of Central Australia today.

One must cross the river at Kerne Bridge to visit Goodrich Castle but, near Walford, a good view of it can be obtained from the river meadows and Figure 56 shows how this twelfth-century castle was built on a river bluff of the Brownstones. It is indeed a wonderful example of how local stone was used to build such massive structure. Figure 57 shows how the castle seems to have grown out of the underlying rocks. Even the moat was carved out of the steeply dipping sandstones, and most probably the excavated slabs of stone were used on the spot for the ramparts and castle walls. Looking northwards from the castle, one can see the spire of Ross church nestling under the foothills forming Chase Wood and Penyard Park. This tabular-shaped hill mass, a very conspicuous topographical feature in this region, is actually a detached fragment of the Forest of Dean plateau and has the same general elevation of 600 feet. The explanation that this hill has been detached as the result of river erosion does not seem so convincing when one observes that the valley between the main plateau of Dean and Chase Wood is occupied by a tiny stream which seems out of all proportion to the size and depth of the valley.

Professor Austin Miller investigated this locality in 1935 and suggested that the valley could have formerly been occupied by the ancient river Wye and the present course of the valley is that of a cut-off meander. The block diagram, Figure 58, shows the suggested course of this 'fossil' meander and the writer convinced himself of the possible truth of this by walking from Cobrey Park through the valley to Frogmore and Weston-under-Penyard to Ross. Southwards from Ross, the old railway line runs along the valley to Tudorville and further on to Walford, and it seems that the neck of the meander was close to the site of the town centre of Ross. When did the Wye finally abandon this valley? Today, the river at Ross is 100 feet above sea level while this flat-floored ancient valley is about 100 feet higher. It is not very easy to show on the block diagram that the course of this meander is on a higher level than the present river Wye, but when one compares it with the levels in the Severn terraces it seems likely that the meander became cut off within the last few thousand years in an interglacial period when the climate was much wetter and

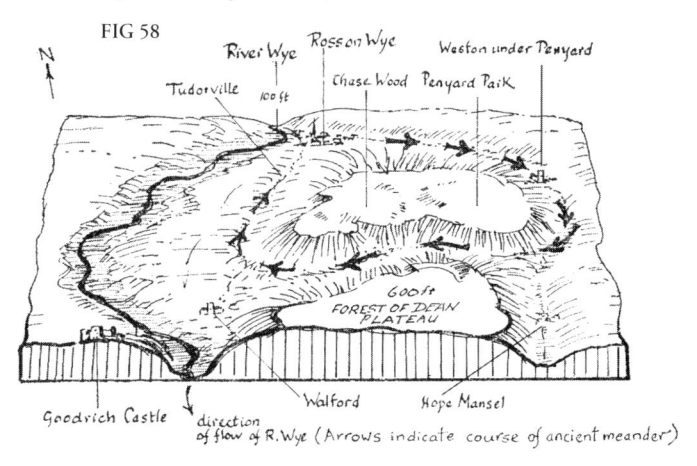

FIG 58

Block diagram showing an ancient meander of the Wye (strata not shown)

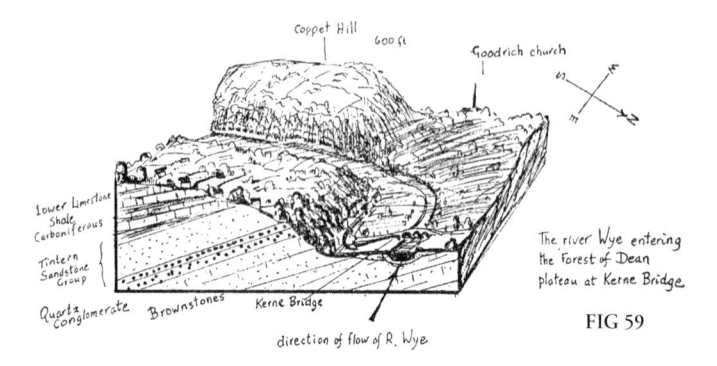

Figure 59 caption labels:
Coppet Hill 600 ft · Goodrich church
Lower Limestone Shale Carboniferous
Tintern Sandstone Group
Quartz Conglomerate · Brownstones · Kerne Bridge
direction of flow of R. Wye
The river Wye entering the Forest of Dean plateau at Kerne Bridge.

FIG 59

the erosive power of rivers much greater. Consulting the one inch to the mile ordnance Survey Map (Sheet 142), one can see a large meander of the Wye between Kings Caple and Foy only two miles upstream from Ross. This meander has an amplitude of more than two miles, which is comparable with the ancient meander mentioned above, and it seems probable that a series of such wide meanders was developed during the same period in the history of the river.

From a few miles above Hereford to Ross the Wye flows across a region which geographers call 'The Plain of Hereford', although really a dissected low plateau of Old Red Sandstone country into which the large meanders of the river are entrenched. In the 25-mile stretch from Hereford to Ross the fall of the river is from 150 feet per mile

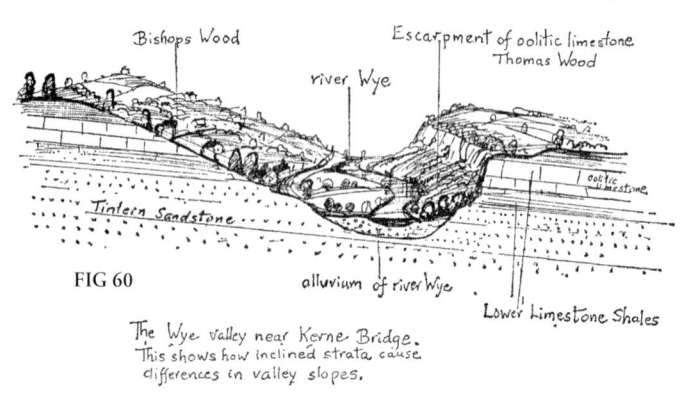

Figure 60 labels:
Bishops Wood · river Wye · Escarpment of oolitic limestone Thomas Wood
Tintern Sandstone · alluvium of river Wye · oolitic limestone · Lower Limestone Shales

FIG 60

The Wye valley near Kerne Bridge. This shows how inclined strata cause differences in valley slopes.

to 100 feet, giving a rate of fall of 2 feet per mile. At Monmouth, the river is 50 feet above sea level and in this 25-mile stretch the fall is 21/2 feet per mile. The gradient of the river obviously varies but this will not help to explain why, after flowing across the plain of Hereford, the Wye decides to reach the sea apparently by the more difficult way through the hard rocks of the Forest of Dean.

The block diagram, Figure 59, shows how the river enters the plateau by Kerne Bridge, creating the picturesque gorge which culminates in the spectacular scenery of the Symond's Yat area. A few hundred yards downstream from the bridge, the river has cut through the resistant band of the Quartz Conglomerate and through the limestones of the Lower Carboniferous series. The strata are dipping transverse to the valley here, so that on one side there is a more gentle slope forming the true dip slope, while on the other side an escarpment is formed. At Thomas Wood, there are precipitous cliffs of oolitic limestone of the Lower Limestone Shale series forming an escarpment with the dip slope on the opposite side, giving an asymmetrical valley (Figure 60). The outstanding topographical feature seen from Kerne Bridge is Coppet Hill, formed by the outcrop of the Quartz Conglomerate and beyond this is Symond's Yat, the finest scenic area of all in the Wye valley and the subject of the next chapter.

Chapter 10
The Symond's Yat Area

ONE of Britain's most famous beauty spots, Symond's Yat is, to use the oft quoted term, 'an area of outstanding natural beauty' and caters for coach trips, campers, canoeists and field centre studies in natural history. Although the hillsides in places are dotted with chalets and cottages, building is now fortunately severely restricted in order to preserve the area's natural amenities. In dealing with the geological background to the scenery here, no geochronological order will be observed, but scenic spots with spectacular rock formations will be described with reference to other areas in the locality where there are similar rocks.

The Wye enters the 'plains' again near Huntsham bridge and after making a sweeping meander re-enters the hard rocks of Dean at Symond's Yat, 'yat' meaning 'gate'. To reach the Symond's Yat Rock, the focal point of all this grand scenery, walkers can either approach from Whitchurch and cross the river by the pretty footbridge at the Biblins, or use either of the two ferries operating at Symond's Yat. Motorists must come into the area over the Huntsham bridge, or by way of Coleford and Berry Hill. The latter is a better route as on this side there are more facilities for parking is well as the amenities of the attractive Log Cabin café, and several 'old world' cottage tea gardens.

With the aid of the direction-finder mounted on a pedestal at Symond's Yat Rock, one can pick out many physical features all of which are related to the geology of the region. In the first place there is the gorge below, with the narrow neck of the meander of which Yat Rock is a relic. There are several theories about the origin of the Wye gorge and its incised meanders but the most convincing one is the following.

In the early Pleistocene period, about two million years ago, when the sea was 600 feet above its present level, the river Wye wandered over a plain with big wide meanders, one of which lies in the panorama to the north of the Rock. Evidence of this former plain can be seen by looking eastwards in the direction of English Bicknor where a general plateau level of 600 feet can be recognised. Sea level has been falling since the Pliocene period and this has caused the river to become far more vigorous, eroding downwards very rapidly to form a valley of ever increasing

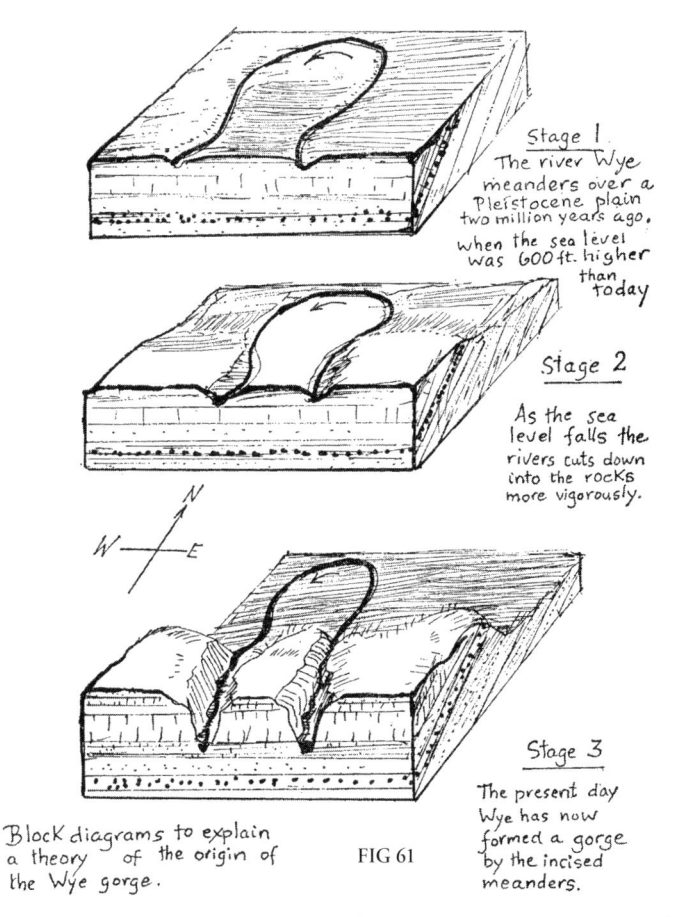

Stage 1. The river Wye meanders over a Pleistocene plain two million years ago, when the sea level was 600 ft. higher than today.

Stage 2. As the sea level falls the rivers cuts down into the rocks more vigorously.

Stage 3. The present day Wye has now formed a gorge by the incised meanders.

Block diagrams to explain a theory of the origin of the Wye gorge.

FIG 61

depth so that the original meanders became entrenched in the ancient plain which today is our plateau of the Forest of Dean. The diagrams in Figure 61 show some of the stages, but the falling sea level was not a continuous downward movement. There were intermittent pauses, and during these standstill periods the river deposited sands and gravels to build up terraces, the remnants of which can be seen in many parts of the Wye valley today, eg, Lancaut peninsula, but of course always

FIG 62 Symonds Yat Rock

Labels on sketch: Yat Rock, Lower Dolomite; Tintern Sandstone; Lower Limestone Shale; Junction of Lower Limestone Shale with Lower Dolomite; old railway line; River Wye; meadow land on alluvium.

above the present flood plain of the river. Other fluctuations of sea level affected the Wye in its lower course and these points will be dealt with in a later chapter. One can from the Stage 3 diagram in Figure 61 that there is an obvious alternative theory and that the Dean plateau could have been formed by being pushed vertically upwards so that the meanders became entrenched in this way. However, when considering this theory one should take into account the evidence offered by the Avon gorge, an area not so very far away.

The sketch, Figure 62, shows that it is possible to reach the narrowest part of the meander neck simply by walking through the old railway tunnel. If the tunnel were twenty times wider, one could divert the river through it and cut off the meander once and for all!

Yat Rock lies on a promontory of Lower Dolomite which has vertical joints, and in such a situation the joints tend to open, causing the formation of craggy cliffs high above the river. The Longstone shown in Figures 63 and 64 is a good example of this. In the past, crags have fallen down into the river below causing rapids. Gradually, silt accumulates and is soon colonised by vegetation so that small islands are formed. These islands then speed up the current in one channel and form rapids, just as the Wye Rapids were formed by the island shown in Figure 63. In other cases, rapids may be formed by resistant bands of rock cropping out on the river bed.

The Lower Dolomite in this area is about 300 feet thick and forms magnificent cliffs on both sides of the river, especially at Coldwell Rocks where the Forestry Commission have made a grand cliff walk, a printed guide to which can be bought at the Log Cabin café. The strata dip 14 degrees due south here, so that further south the Lower Dolomite cliffs come right down to the river banks in the Biblins area. However, structures are not everywhere the same, and at Rosemary Topping, half a mile north-east of Coldwell Rocks, a small synclinal structure has formed a steep hill which towers

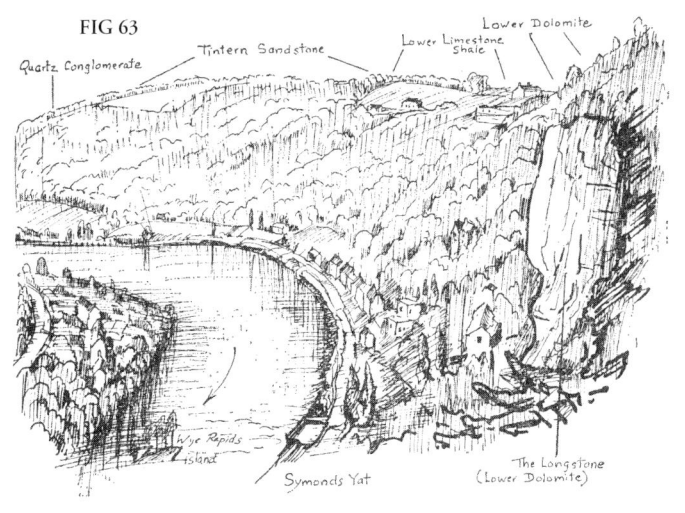

FIG 63

Labels: Quartz Conglomerate, Tintern Sandstone, Lower Limestone Shale, Lower Dolomite, Wye Rapids Island, Symonds Yat, The Longstone (Lower Dolomite)

magnificently above the river as shown Figure 65. Anticlines tend to be weak structures and although one might think that an upfold would form a mountain, it is the syncline with its closer packed joints that is more resistant to erosion. Snowdon, for instance, is a mountain with a synclinal structure.

Dolomite, as we have seen, is a kind of limestone; actually, a marine rock laid down in the Carboniferous seas some 320 million years ago but under different conditions from those in the seas today. Dolomite limestones have also been formed in other geological periods. Dolomite is an admixture of approximately equal amounts of calcium and magnesium carbonates, represented by the chemical formula $(CaMg)CO_3$. It is believed that limestones were laid down in the first place but that, soon after compaction, chemical changes produced a dolomite rock which, according to chemical analysis, contains an average of 30 per cent CaO, 22 per cent of MgO and 48 per cent of CO_2. This chemical change is known as 'dolomitisation', but it is patchy so that in some places the rock is a pure limestone while in others a denser rock is formed producing many small cracks and shrinkage cavities. This can be seen if one clambers down to examine the face of Yat Rock – the best approach being from the road lower down, or any of the Lower Dolomite cliffs bordering the river.

FIG 64

Longstone – a detached block of Lower Dolomite

Lower Limestone Shale

Symonds Yat

FIG 65

Synclinal structure
Dip ← → Dip
R. Wye

Rosemary Topping
a small synclinal structure in Lower Dolomite

The mineral dolomite is denser and harder than calcite so that crushed dolomite is a much more suitable material for motorways than crushed limestone; hence the importance of such dolomite quarries as those in the Tidenham and Chepstow areas. Unfortunately, in the dolomitisation process the structures of fossils, such as crinoids, corals and brachiopods, tend to be destroyed so that it is only in odd patches that the observant can recognise the vestiges of fossils. In places there are cavities known as 'geodes' which are occupied by layers of calcite crystals. However, the geologist can test for dolomite in the field by applying drops of dilute hydrochloric acid; a very weak fizz (effervescence) or none at all proves the rock to be a dolomite, while vigorous effervescence proves that the lump of rock being examined is either limestone or a calcareous rock. Throughout the area, the Lower Dolomite has a uniform colour of pinkish grey with here and there blood-red streaks, the colouring mineral being haematite, or ferric oxide.

The Crease Limestone lies above the Lower Dolomite outcrop quite close to the cliff top but a few hundred yards south of Yat Rock, a little way down the road under the footbridge, the open textured Crease Limestone has been worked for pockets of iron ore and traces of thinly crusted haematite can still be seen in some of the cavities.

The view northwards from Yat Rock to Huntsham and Coppet Hills is shown in Figure 66 and the outcrop of the Quartz Conglomerate can be easily picked out on both hills by the fallen blocks, many of them a thousand tons in weight, lying scattered in the field. Owing to the southerly dip, the Conglomerate comes down to the river on both sides of the great meander, but even when the outcrop is several hundred feet above the river great masses of rock still tumble down into the water. One such enormous block close to the Ferry Inn, shown in Figure 67, will give canoeists some idea of the hazards to be expected in places where they can see this outcrop on the hillside. The block diagram, Figure 68, shows the sequence of strata laid out before us in this view northwards from the Rock. It will be seen that the first change of slope occurs with the outcrop of the Lower Limestone Shale forming the very base of the Carboniferous Limestone series, which here consist of well-developed limestones with subordinate shales. The acid test can be used to detect the limestones but they can also be

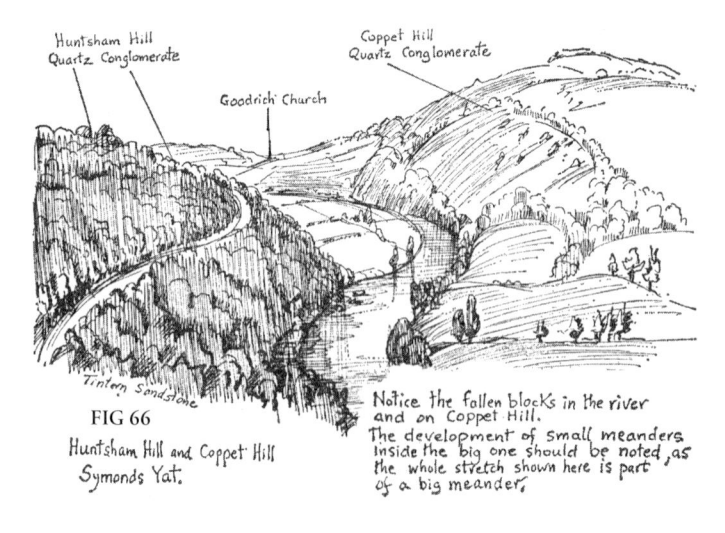

FIG 66
Huntsham Hill and Coppet Hill Symonds Yat.

Notice the fallen blocks in the river and on Coppet Hill.
The development of small meanders inside the big one should be noted, as the whole stretch shown here is part of a big meander.

fallen block of the Quartz Conglomerate by the Ferry Inn Symonds Yat

FIG 67

easily recognised by the abundance of crinoid remains and brachiopods. Close to the old lime kilns on the roadside a few hundred yards north of Yat Rock, there is a disused quarry which can be approached across a field immediately behind the chapel on Yat Rock hill. In small folds revealed here it is possible to see how strong and weak beds react to the folding, but the best exposure of all in the Lower Limestone Shale is at Hadnock Quarry on the bank of the river opposite Little Doward. This quarry was worked until quite recently and is an excellent place for collecting specimens of 'chondrites', a trace fossil (Figure 69).

The block diagram, Figure 68, also shows that a much more subdued relief with open fields marks the outcrop of the Tintern Sandstone group which can be seen en route as we follow a public footpath to Huntsham hill, for here, close to the edge of the Forest, is the Junction of the Carboniferous Lower Limestone Shales with the Devonian Tintern Sandstone. At Huntsham Hill, we can see one of the finest and most extensive exposures of the Quartz Conglomerate in the whole region, for in the woods on the north-eastern side great crags border the escarpment and huge tumbled blocks are strewn in the fields below. This rock, which forms the base of the Upper Devonian, can be studied easily and in great detail here. It consists of white pebbles of vein quartz which are very conspicuous and in sharp contrast to the almost

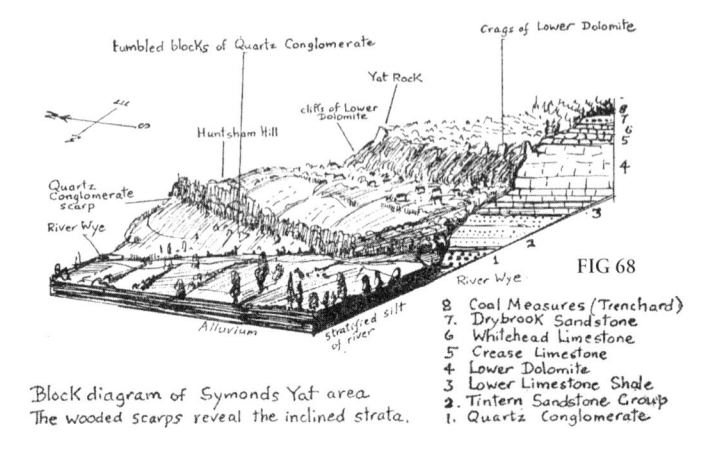

Block diagram of Symonds Yat area.
The wooded scarps reveal the inclined strata.

FIG 68

8. Coal Measures (Trenchard)
7. Drybrook Sandstone
6. Whitehead Limestone
5. Crease Limestone
4. Lower Dolomite
3. Lower Limestone Shale
2. Tintern Sandstone Group
1. Quartz Conglomerate

black pebbles of decomposed igneous rocks. Some pebbles are of quartzite and sandstone but occasionally one can discover blood-red pebbles of the semi-precious stone, jasper. The jaspers here are difficult to get out as they are firmly embedded with a siliceous cement into a sandy matrix.

The outstanding feature of the rock here is the strongly developed vertical joints, which tend to gape much more on promontory escarpments than elsewhere so that weathering along the joints accelerates the tumble downhill.

One of the Forest's 'wonder rocks' is the Suckstone, which may be seen on a well-marked forest pain between Staunton and Mailscot Wood. Its weight is estimated to be 30,000 tons and it is said to be the largest fallen block in all Britain. The sketch of this rock in Figure 70 should be compared with the actual outcrop of the Quartz Conglomerate from which blocks have fallen a few hundred yards downhill, shown in Figure 71. The exposure here at Near Hearkening Rock is just as spectacular as those on Huntsham and Coppet Hills, but the cross-bedding is more marked and, owing to the high dip of 40 degrees, one can obtain better views of the upper and lower surfaces of the bedding planes.

The hill mass of Great Doward is fringed by the scarp of the Quartz Conglomerate which has been cut into by the Wye by the Ferry Inn, and the outcrop is visible in cliffs close to the river bank. This area is rather closely settled with cottages commanding grand views of the Wye gorge, but access should be made on foot as the numerous steep and narrow paths intertwine all over the hill.

The next place of major interest is the Biblins, which can be reached by following the path along the riverside from the old Symond's Yat railway station. It follows the foot of the great cliffs of Lower Dolomite with their almost overhanging crags, to the finely constructed suspension bridge which leads to the Biblins on the opposite bank. This is a popular camping centre, very crowded during weekends and holidays, and the recently constructed field centre in this beauty spot emphasises its importance as a region for studying aspects of natural history, including geology.

Owing to the inclination of the strata, the Crease Limestone which is above the Lower Dolomite comes close to the river here, and being an open-textured limestone with many gaping vertical joints, it forms good cave country. In limestones, surface water percolates through the joints which are widened by solution, thus forming underground rivers and caves. The old explanation of this was that rainwater became acid by absorbing carbon dioxide in its passage through the air, but as the amount of CO_2 in the air is only about 0.02 per cent there must be some other explanation of the acid conditions which are sufficient to dissolve the limestone. In the process of decomposition of

FIG 69

Hadnock Quarry
Carboniferous Limestone
Lower Limestone Shale

plants, soil bacteria create organic acids which attack the limestone and produce the soluble calcium bicarbonate which is then deposited as calcium carbonate in the form of layers of growth on the walls of caves or in between the joints. This is known as 'travertine' and by knocking out a small section one can see the concentric layers of growth. Pinnacle-like deposits on the cave roof, formed by dripping water, are termed stalactites, while stalagmites are built up from the floor, and anyone interested in geology should certainly visit Dropping Wells, in the large cave close to the Biblins, where all these features can be seen in the Lower Dolomite, together with large masses of tufa formed where the redeposited calcium carbonate has petrified much of the vegetation. Here it is possible to find petrified leaves and twigs that have taken only five or ten years to form, whereas the very thick masses of travertine on the cave walls and rock surfaces could be many thousands of years old. (See Figure 73 for explanations of the various features.)

An easy footpath from the Biblins leads to the Seven Sisters Rocks, seven bluffs of limestone which are used nearly every weekend by rock-climbing groups from many parts of Britain. The sketch, Figure 72, helps to explain their formation, for it can be seen that the Crease Limestone dips rather steeply towards the river and this tends to open the joints and even to cause blocks to tumble

The Suckstone
A fallen block of the Quartz Conglomerate

FIG 70

FIG 71

Near Hearkening Rock. The Quartz Conglomerate dipping at 40°

into the water. Close examination of this white limestone reveals that it is composed of tiny ooliths each only a few hundredths of an inch in diameter and so minute that a lens is necessary to see them. The ooliths in the Cotswold limestones are much larger. Each oolith consists of concentric layers of calcium carbonate around a minute grain. Their exact origin is not fully understood, although there is no doubt that they can be mechanically formed on the floor of the sea by current action, ie, by the grain being rolled along and gathering layers of calcium carbonate. However, it has been suggested more recently that microscopic algae could have led to their formation. The weathered surfaces of this oolite often show current bedding, which provides one clue as to their origin.

The sketch, Figure 72, shows a remarkable feature of these limestone bluffs, that they are undercut in a way which suggests that the river Wye was responsible when it was flowing at a higher level, even though all the bluffs are not at the same altitude. These bare limestone crags are covered with lichens, so that when it rains the water travels from the top of the pedestal to the bottom where is constantly forming 'drip tips'. The water, which has been made acid by the organic residues of the lichens covering the rock surface, drains down under the foot of the pedestal

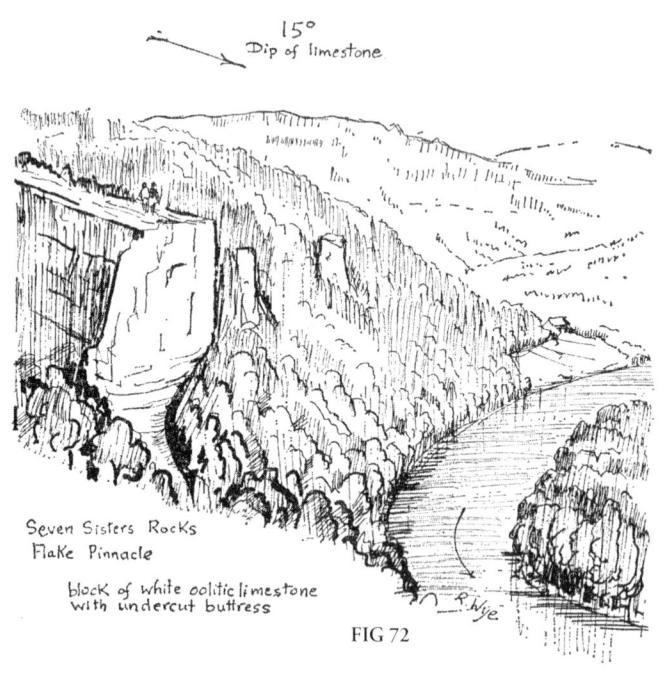

Figure 72 labels:
- 15° Dip of limestone
- Seven Sisters Rocks Flake Pinnacle
- block of white oolitic limestone with undercut buttress
- R. Wye

FIG 72

and is probably responsible for the undercut buttress. (See Figure 73 Section A.) The travertine-coated surfaces bear witness to this in many cases.

On the limestone plateau above the Seven Sisters the natural vegetation consists of lime-loving plants, eg, the Brachypodium or Tor Grass and Erect Brome, grasses typical of limestone areas. If one examines the rock surface underlying the soil in the limestone plateau areas of Great Doward, one can see that the surfaces between the joints, known as clints, are smooth with many depressions and fluted channels very similar to those on the limestone pavements at Malham in the Northern Pennines. This evidence suggests that the weathering of limestones is mostly biological, or we could say 'biogenic'. The organic residues derived from plants in the soil cover are oxidised by micro-organisms, which set free the organic acids that dissolve the limestone pavements, so producing depressions and widening the vertical joints. Scenery of this kind, developed in limestone areas of the world, is called karst topography.

King Arthur's cave, which lies on the western side of Great Doward, is one of a series developed in a band of limestone known as the Crease Limestone. The floor of this cave has been excavated and the various layers indicate periods of occupation beginning some 20,000 years ago during the Ice Age. Evidence suggests that the cave has been occupied by Upper Palaeolithic Man (Aurignacian), Mesolithic, Neolithic and Bronze Age people. The oldest deposits, eleven feet below the present surface, have yielded the bones of cave bear, lion, hyena, rhinoceros, mammoth, giant Irish deer, bison, reindeer and horse. Some of the finds of this cave are now in the small museum at Monmouth, but as yet there is no authoritative explanation of the origin of the cave. It is easy to imagine that the river Wye once flowed near to this cave and there is doubt that the caves in this area were formed at a period when the climate was much wetter and the water table much higher in the limestones than it is today. Some of the caves are almost sealed up with rock debris and still await investigation. Merlin's Cave in the Crease Limestone on the other side of Great Doward, near cliffs overlooking the river, has been much altered by iron miners who followed the Crease Limestone in their quest for ore.

The plateau of Great Doward is capped with Drybrook Sandstone and if we follow the forestry road

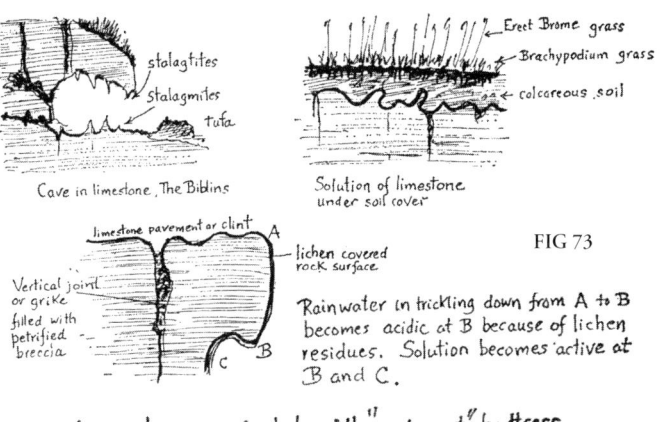

FIG 73

Cave in limestone, The Biblins — stalagtites, stalagmites, tufa

Solution of limestone under soil cover — Erect Brome grass, Brachypodium grass, calcareous soil

Limestone pedestal with "undercut" buttress. — limestone pavement or clint A, lichen covered rock surface, Vertical joint or grike filled with petrified breccia, C, B

Rainwater in trickling down from A to B becomes acidic at B because of lichen residues. Solution becomes active at B and C.

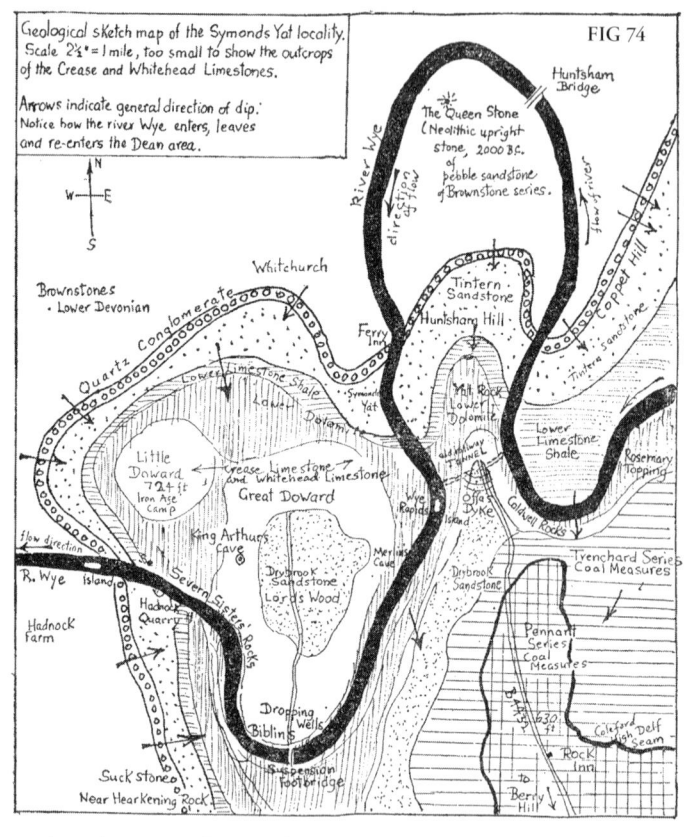

Geology Explained in the Forest of Dean and Wye Valley

FIG 74

Geological sketch map of the Symonds Yat locality. Scale 2½" = 1 mile, too small to show the outcrops of the Crease and Whitehead Limestones.

Arrows indicate general direction of dip. Notice how the river Wye enters, leaves and re-enters the Dean area.

[Sketch map showing: River Wye, Huntsham Bridge, The Queen Stone (Neolithic upright stone, 2000 B.C. of pebble sandstone of Brownstone series), Brownstones Lower Devonian, Whitchurch, Quartz Conglomerate, Tintern Sandstone, Huntsham Hill, Ferry Inn, Coppet Hill, Lower Limestone Shale, Symonds Yat, Mill Rock Lower Dolomite, Lower Dolomite, Little Doward 724 ft Iron Age Camp, Crease Limestone and Whitehead Limestone, Great Doward, Wye Rapids, Offa's Dyke, Rosemary Topping, Coldwell Rocks, King Arthur's Cave, Merlin's Cave, Trenchard Series Coal Measures, Severn Sisters' Rocks, Hadnock Quarry, Drybrook Sandstone, Lord's Wood, Drybrook Sandstone, Pennant Series Coal Measures, Hadnock farm, Dropping Wells, Biblins, Suspension Footbridge, Rock Inn, Coleford High Delf Seam, Suck stones, Near Hearkening Rock, Berry Hill]

northwards to Lords Wood we can easily see the change from limestone, for where the sandy soils with scattered blocks of sandstone are visible in roadside cuttings, the presence of underlying sandstone is revealed. Also, the vegetation changes from calcareous-loving plants to those preferring the more acid soils. About a quarter of a mile north of King Arthur's Cave is an active quarry in the Crease Limestone which here is a white oolite and is crushed to make agricultural lime. The adjacent hill of Little Doward towers up to a height of 724 feet above the river and here we are coming to the rim

The Symond's Yat Area

of the Dean plateau. The tumbled crags of the Quartz Conglomerate outcrop again, just above the picturesque mansion of Wyastone Leys, where the Wye once more makes its exit from Dean.

Before concluding this chapter on this most famous beauty spot, mention must be made of a small area immediately to the south of Symond's Yat Rock. Close to the car park, there are a series of concentric earthwork banks and ditches known as Offa's Dyke, but although Offa, the Mercian king, used the ramparts in the eighth century AD, for the demarcation zone between the Welsh and the English, it was really constructed during the Iron Age, about 200 BC, and is typical of the promontory hill forts which are also seen in the Cotswold escarpment and at Herefordshire Beacon. The builders must have known their local geology for most of the rampart is of the very suitable Drybrook Sandstone which crops out here. (The Queen Stone close to the river and at the northern tip of the great meander core is of Lower Devonian sandstone and believed to be Neolithic.)

Following a forestry road south of Offa's Dyke, we find a marked sandstone feature a few hundred yards south of the car park. This marks the boundary of the Forest of Dean coalfield. Of the many thousands visitors who come here every week, very few realise that amid all this grand scenery is an old coal mine, though the blue-grey shales denoting an old pit heap are clearly visible from the road close to the well-known Rock Inn. It has often been stated that the Forest of Dean coalfield is one of the prettiest in Britain because it is so well concealed by forests, but here the open fields are on the outcrop of the Coal Measures and there is a rise of the land to 600 feet. There is nearly always a distinct scarp feature where the Trenchard series of the Coal Measures are adjacent to the sandstones of the Pennant series, for the latter give rise to higher ground. It is this topographical feature which helped miners to locate the richest coal seam of all, the Coleford High Delf seam, which crops out at the foot of this scarp just to the east of the Rock Inn. Visitors who follow the recommended forest walk from Yat Rock along the Coldwell Rocks will find that the swampy ground with numerous springs occurs just where the Coal Measures, with their clays and shales at the base, rest on the Crease Limestone. Geological sketch map, Figure 74, shows the location of most of the places mentioned in this chapter, but to explore the area thoroughly the Ordnance Survey Map, Sheet SO51, on the scale of 2½ inches to the mile, is essential.

Chapter 11

The Wye Valley: Monmouth Area

THE river Wye once more makes its exit from the Forest of Dean between the high, rugged hill of Little Doward and Hadnock Quarry. High up above the castle-like mansion of Wyastone Leys, we can see the turreted crags of the Quartz Conglomerate, as if signalling to the canoeist that the hazards of the rapids in the gorge are for the time being over. And now, with Hadnock Farm on the left, the meadowlands open out into the 'plains' round Monmouth. Unfortunately, for the last three years the peaceful solitude which sent Wordsworth into poetic raptures has been broken by the noise of giant caterpillar tractors and huge excavating machines at work upon the new motorway. It has been no easy task for here, on the main road close to Wyastone Leys and only about two miles from Monmouth, the builders came up against a geological problem of sufficient magnitude to have caused a greatly increased burden to the taxpayer. This chapter will be mainly devoted to the problem, for although the aim of the book is to demonstrate geology through scenery, the importance of applied geology to civil engineering deserves emphasis.

The block diagram, Figure 75, shows that at this particular locality both road and river run almost along the strike of the Lower Devonian rocks, and it can be seen that the strata dip transversely to, and towards, the road and river. The plateau of Hayes Coppice may be a remnant of the Dean plateau but its edge abuts on to the road, so that the builders must of necessity excavate into it when making a modem motorway.

Owing to the objections of local landowners and other interests, the new carriageway had to be located in a cutting. Here, the strata consist of massive sandstones dipping at an angle of 30 degrees. Some of these sandstones are up to fifteen feet in thickness but, interbedded with them, are thin layers of sandy, micaceous shales and thin beds of red and green marls. There has always been a tendency here for masses to slip downhill to the river banks but before the days of the motorway construction, a large mass slipped down to the river carrying with it a number of trees. This 'forest on the move' came to rest by the river and is shown in Figure 75, so the warning was already there before operations began.

The problem became more apparent when excavations were made for the construction of the new trunk road, and a considerable

FIG 75

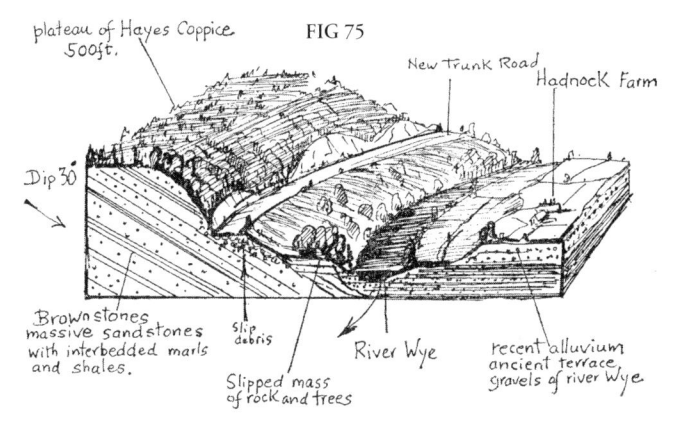

- plateau of Hayes Coppice. 500ft.
- New Trunk Road
- Hadnock Farm
- Dip 30°
- Brownstones massive sandstones with interbedded marls and shales.
- slip debris
- Slipped mass of rock and trees
- River Wye
- recent alluvium ancient terrace, gravels of river Wye

The great civil engineering problem on the new Trunk Road between Monmouth and Ross

amount of vegetation cover on the slopes of Hayes Coppice Wood was removed, exposing the bare rock surface to the weather. During heavy rainfall, the water soaked away very quickly into the joints in the sandstones and worked its way down to the beds of marl. This provided a fine lubricated surface beneath the massive sandstones, which then began to push downhill even more rapidly. Rock masses began to slide down on to the road and on one occasion in 1964 the road had to be closed for three days as it had suddenly sunk four to six feet. This was due to another man-made catastrophe. Great masses of the excavated rock had been dumped on the river side of the new highway to create an embankment to support the lower carriageway but, as shown in Figure 76, it provided no support at all as it rested on thick layers of river silt.

Down by the river, this unconsolidated alluvium began to heave up and so a subsoil movement began and the carriageway continued to sink. It was the weight of this embankment, not the slipping of the rock masses, which caused the unconsolidated alluvium in the river to heave. The Ministry of Transport asked for a report and this was given by a geologist specialising in soil mechanics, a branch of civil engineering and geology which is becoming of great importance today in the construction of modem roads, bridges and barrages. In this Monmouth section of the

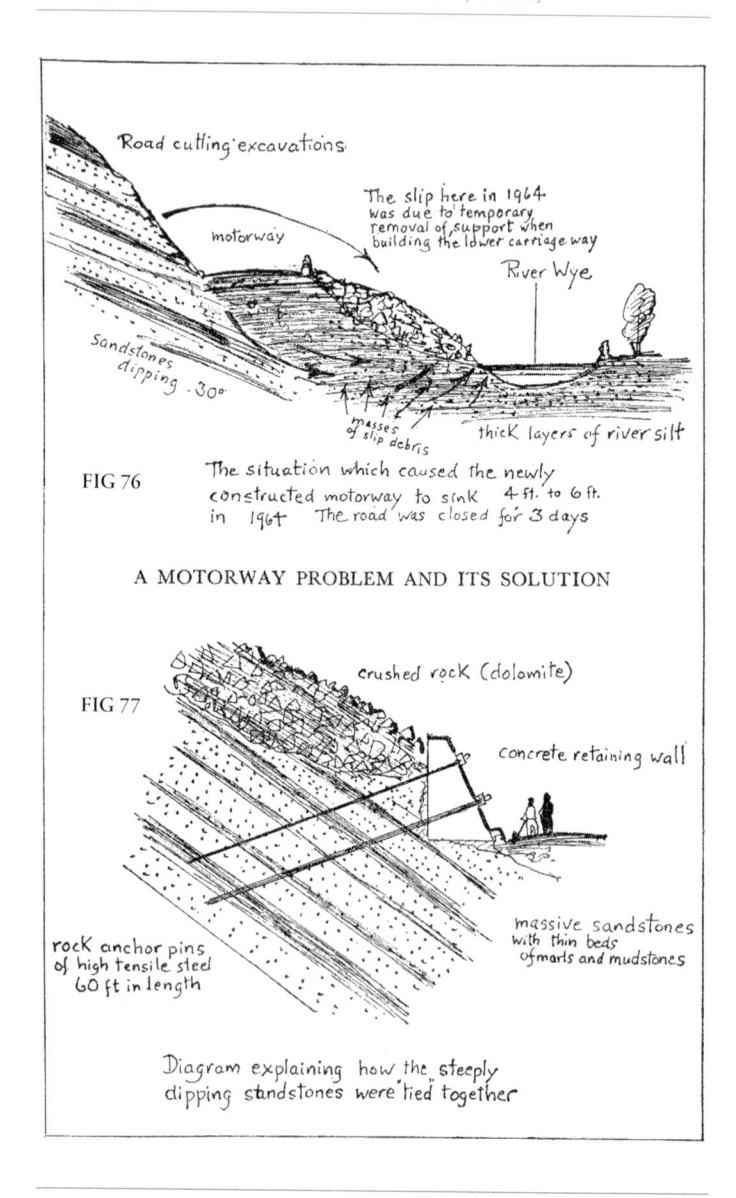

Geology Explained in the Forest of Dean and Wye Valley

FIG 76 — Road cutting excavations. motorway. The slip here in 1964 was due to temporary removal of support when building the lower carriage way. River Wye. Sandstones dipping 30°. masses of slip debris. thick layers of river silt.

The situation which caused the newly constructed motorway to sink 4 ft. to 6 ft. in 1964. The road was closed for 3 days.

A MOTORWAY PROBLEM AND ITS SOLUTION

FIG 77 — crushed rock (dolomite). concrete retaining wall. rock anchor pins of high tensile steel 60 ft in length. massive sandstones with thin beds of marls and mudstones.

Diagram explaining how the steeply dipping sandstones were "tied" together.

The Wye Valley: Monmouth Area

A40 carriageway, known as Leys Bend, there were two problems, the downhill movement of the sandstones on to the roadway and the sinking of the road a few hundred yards further away. Special rock anchor pins, each sixty feet in length, were driven into the hillside in an attempt to 'fasten' the strata together. The pins were made of special high-tensile steel and pinned to a strong concrete retaining wall, special precautions having been taken to avoid corrosion of the metal by weather. The rods tying the sandstones together were not alone sufficient. In addition, the bare rock surfaces on the hillside were covered with crushed rock (dolomite from the Chepstow quarries), which will later be concreted over to minimise the downward movement of water into the marl layers. A rough impression of the problem is given in Figure 77.

The other problem was solved by constructing drains to relieve pore-pressure in the silts and by the use of 'gabions'. These are wire baskets filled with crushed rock and tied together, all the wires being carefully coated with plastic material. This idea originated in Italy and these baskets have been very successful in the construction of autostrada in the Alps, flood control embankments

Leys Bend, on the A.40 road near Monmouth. The creation of two carriage ways gives a terrace effect. The separation of the carriage way was necessary owing to the steep topography.

FIG 78

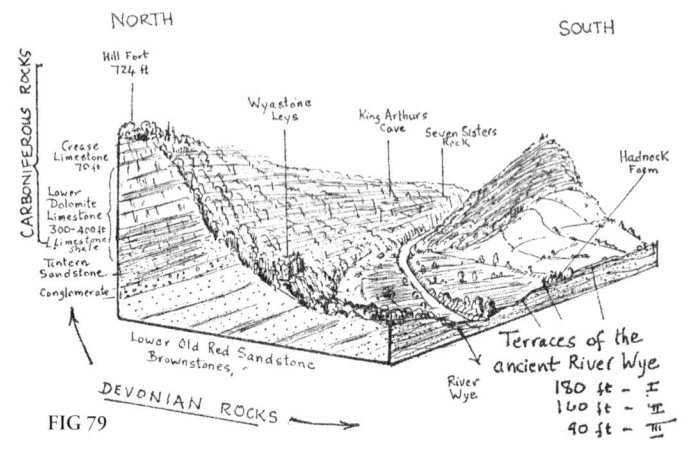

Geology Explained in the Forest of Dean and Wye Valley

FIG 79

(Figure labels: NORTH — SOUTH; CARBONIFEROUS ROCKS: Hill Fort 724 ft, Crease Limestone 70 ft, Lower Dolomite Limestone 300-400 ft, Limestone shale, Tintern Sandstone, Conglomerate, Wyastone Leys, King Arthurs Cave, Seven Sisters Rock, Hadnock Farm; DEVONIAN ROCKS: Lower Old Red Sandstone Brownstones; River Wye; Terraces of the ancient River Wye 180 ft – I, 160 ft – II, 90 ft – III)

arid piers. The gabion basket is an attempt to partially consolidate rock waste and to do so quickly, whereas the natural process would take something like a million years. Figure 78 shows how the separation of the carriageways was dictated by the configuration of the ground, the steep slopes being the result of the steeply dipping sandstones. It has been suggested that the contractors might have encountered fewer geological problems had they been less solicitous of the surface objectors, but at the time decisions had to be taken these objectors were voluble and vociferous, while the rocks had yet to speak.

South of Leys Bend, great care had to be taken not to disturb the sandstones beds as they lie, since any movement there would have led to disaster.

Referring again to Figure 75 and also to Figure 79, we can see that the river has built up terraces of older alluvium that are now found well above its present level. Thus Hadnock Farm is situated some thirty feet above the river on an ancient terrace, and the Wye here is at sixty feet above sea level. This can be proved by examining gravels and silt in the various fields around this farm. Such well-drained soils above meadows which are liable to winter flooding provide very good arable land. However, the most fertile soils in the whole region are those derived from the St Maughan's group of rocks in the Lower Devonian. This group consists of interbedded marls and sandstones, but in the Monmouth area there are many bands of limestones, thus providing good calcareous soils which are also rich in iron from the red sandstones.

A remarkable sandstone relief feature occurs on the left bank of the Wye opposite the town of Monmouth, where steeply rising hills form the locality known as the Kymin. Like the Symond's Yat area, it is rather closely settled and dotted all over this hillside are numerous cottages commanding excellent views of the 'plains of Monmouth'. The best views are from the Naval Temple on the summit, which is capped by a rather wide outcrop of the Quartz Conglomerate. Here, too, it is easy to see the variations in relief controlled by the outcrop of the Lower Devonian, the undulating plains on the St Maughan's group at 100 to 150 feet, followed by a sharp rise on to the sandstones of the Brownstones at 400 to 500 feet, with a capping of the resistant Quartz Conglomerate at 800 feet forming the crest of the Kymin.

Chapter 12

The Wye Valley: Monmouth to Tintern Abbey

ONE mile south of Monmouth, the river Wye once more re-enters the Dean plateau but this is for the last time as the next escape is to the Severn estuary at Chepstow. Figure 80 shows the great scarp formed by the Brownstones and the Quartz Conglomerate at Livox Wood. The quiet, secluded village of Penalt, situated at the top of the scarp, is an excellent viewpoint overlooking the gateway into Dean, for the Wye valley is now a highway for the main road to Chepstow via Tintern Abbey. The fertile plains of Monmouth now give place to another gorge section resembling in a smaller way the Rhine gorge from Bingen to Bonn, since both are incised in a plateau.

Great emphasis has been laid in all the previous chapters on the way in which the scenery is controlled by the different rocks and their varying resistance to weathering. There are, however, many features of scenery that cannot be related only to this but can partly be explained in terms of the recent history of the Wye, and by recent we mean in the last two million years! For example, a very fine view of the Wye gorge can be seen from near the Pludds and in the sketch, Figure 81, we can see quite clearly that the scene is one of plateaux at different levels. The dominant plateau in this view is 500 feet high and the Wye has entrenched itself into this. Many thousands of years

FIG 80

The river re-enters the Forest of Dean plateau near Monmouth.

FIG 81

View of the Wye terraces from The Pludds

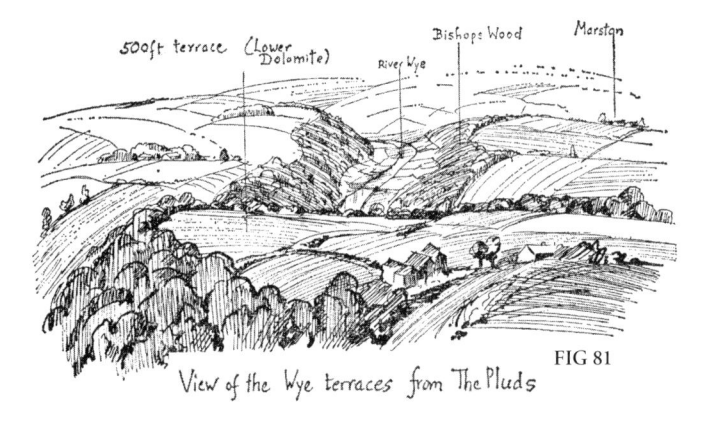

(Labels on figure: 500ft terrace (Lower Dolomite); River Wye; Bishops Wood; Marstan)

ago the plain of the river was also at 500 feet. Later, the river became much more vigorous and started cutting into its plain, so making the gorge which is such a striking feature today. By geomorphologists, the process is termed rejuvenation of the river. The edges of the plateau shown in Figure 81 mark the stages of rejuvenation which could have been caused by a falling sea level. This scene is not in the locality of this chapter but it is brought in as the view from the Pludds is a very convincing one.

It is significant that throughout the entire region the finest scenery is at the junction of the Devonian with the Carboniferous rocks, which in turn provide great variety within a small area. Such a location is Staunton, a pretty village where the main tourist attraction is the Buckstone. The block diagram, Figure 82, indicates that the 'stone' is a crag on the escarpment of the Quartz Conglomerate, which here reaches its highest point at 915 feet on Staunton Meend. Here, again, we can see the strong geological control in the landscape, the vale being in the softer rocks of the Tintern Sandstone group with ridges on either side formed by the Conglomerate and the Lower Dolomite; the village of Staunton itself lies on a limestone ridge in the Lower Limestone Shale division of the Lower Carboniferous. It is from this viewpoint of the Buckstone that the core of the Newland meander can be seen as shown in Figure 83. This is one of the largest abandoned meander channels in the whole of the river Wye but if we examine the map of the river from Monmouth to Tintern the very absence of typical meanders leads us to suspect that they were there once upon a time but have now been cut off.

Not far from the village of Newland there is an excellent view of the abandoned channel from near Lodges Barn, as shown in the sketch, Figure 84. Here we have a deep valley occupied by a tiny trickle of a stream. In fact, on arriving at this viewpoint, a party of ramblers looking for the river once proclaimed that this was the Wye valley, not having noticed that the rather flat-floored valley contained no river. The sketch map, Figure 85, shows the great extent of this fossil meander, which provides quite an interesting four-mile circular ramble beginning at Redbrook and finishing up only a quarter of a mile from the starting point. The neck of the meander must have been cut off and the channel abandoned quite a long time ago compared with the Ross meander, for this valley is 370 feet above the present level of

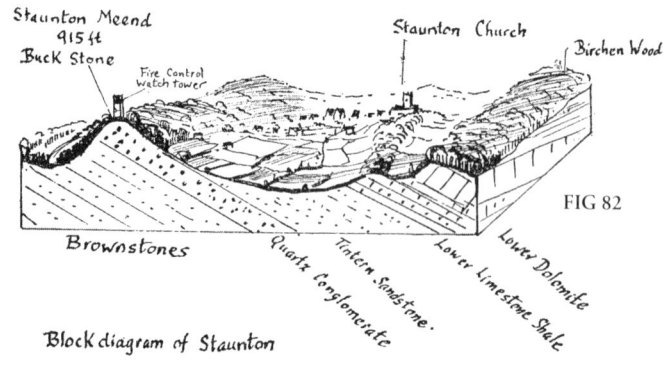

Block diagram of Staunton — FIG 82

the Wye at Redbrook. The block diagram, Figure 86, shows how the core of the meander is really an isolated remnant of the Dean plateau at 500 to 600 feet. Both Highbury Plain and Astridge Barn are fine examples of erosion platforms, their remarkably flat nature being due to a capping of thin limestones of the Lower Carboniferous (Figure 87). The slow weathering of limestones by solution tends to produce such a feature. It must be noted that because the limestones in this case are nearly horizontal it need not be an erosion platform. Most of Wales is made up of plateaux at different levels into which have been carved deep valleys made deeper by glaciers of the recent past. Most of the land forms in Britain have been sculptured in the last two million years, the Wye valley being no exception.

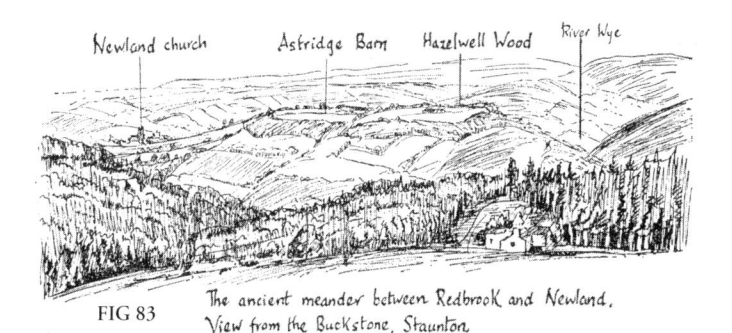

FIG 83 — The ancient meander between Redbrook and Newland. View from the Buckstone, Staunton.

The flat-floored valleys became a series of swamps when the river was cut off and later, when the land was drained, it became good pasture for dairy cows. As routeways they are, of course, useless, but the sequestered vales are ideal for the rambler desiring to get off the beaten tracks. Recently the large town of Coleford has used the floor of the Newland meander valley for a large sewage works scheme. With the increasing population of the Wye and Dean regions the problems of human waste and town refuse disposal are serious, and to preserve salmon and trout fishing care must be taken to ensure that the Wye does not become polluted.

The last example of a deserted meander is at St Briavels. Here, from the Old Red Sandstone walls

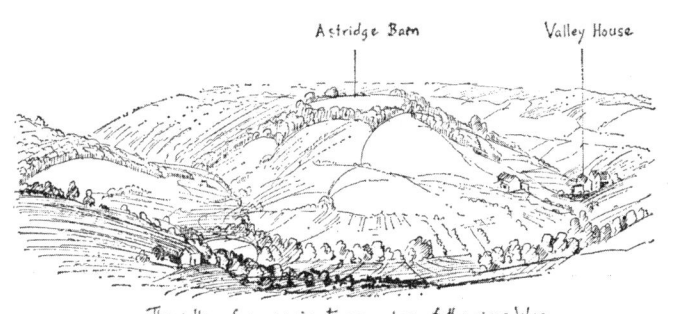

FIG 84 — The valley of an ancient meander of the river Wye near Newland. View from Lodges Barn. The river once flowed through this valley from right to left in the sketch. This valley has now only a tiny stream.

FIG 85

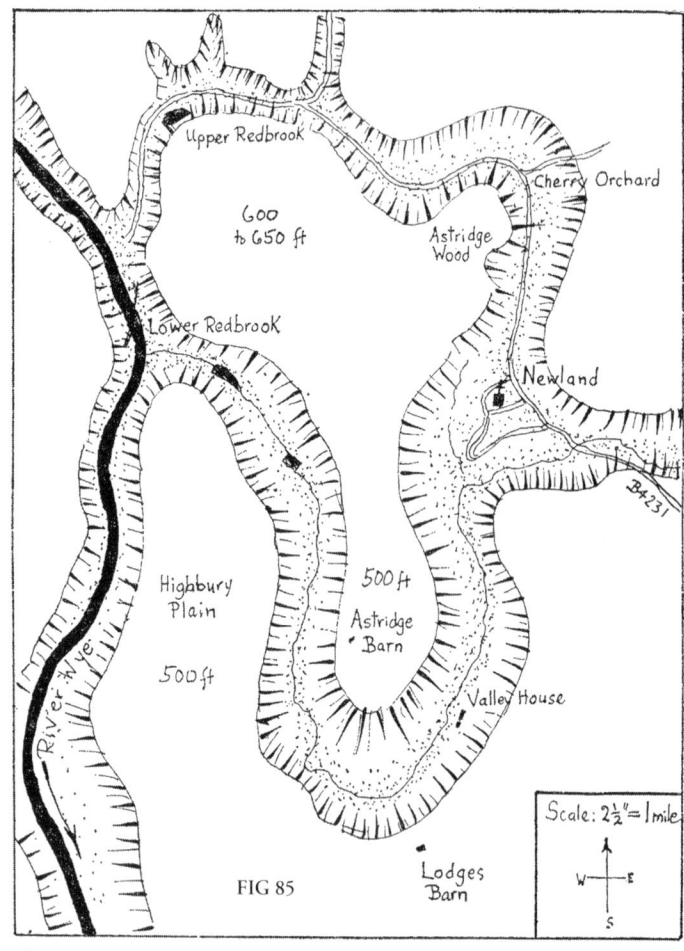

of the twelfth-century castle, we can occupy the top gallery seat of a vast amphitheatre, carved out by the river perhaps much more recently than the Newland meander. For, as shown in Figure 88, the plain across which the ancient Wye flowed is only 100 feet above the river at Bigsweir. We can walk almost half-way round the top circle of our amphitheatre and enjoy grand views of the distant Wye, now flowing below the level of the plain beneath us. This scene is perhaps more convincing than the Newland meander because here Nature has provided a theatre with the platform below, but the main actor, the Wye, has gone off stage. The block diagram, Figure 89, shows that Lindors Farm is at the centre of the meander core. Rambling along the roads and footpaths here one can see gravels and silts in the fields and small exposures on the roadside; true evidence that the river has been here. The soils of the farm area are of typical Wye silt and in fields recently ploughed it is easy to recognise gravels which prove that a fairly large, swift river once flowed at this level. Evidence like this is essential to support any theories as to the origin of the scenery. The whole meander core can be viewed from the hills above Llandogo on the opposite side of the Wye valley, the castle and church of St Briavels standing very clearly on the skyline, like sentinels watching over the plains below (Figure 90).

Has this meander core been put to any use? Beyond doubt, the fertility of Lindors Farm soils is a gift of the Wye, and in more recent times the upper seats of our amphitheatre have been colonised by those wishing to have chalets and cottages with views, for almost every room in every house has a pleasant outlook. The youth hostel at the Castle reminds us of the German 'schloss' on a rocky crag overlooking the Rhine to which ramblers come to rest for the night. Finally, one

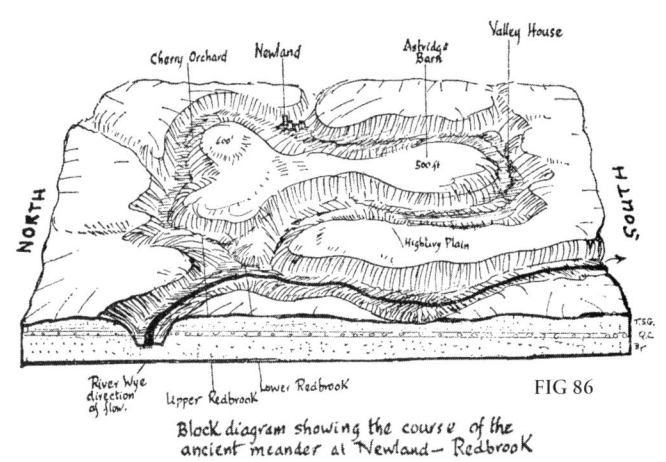

FIG 86

Block diagram showing the course of the ancient meander at Newland–Redbrook

Panoramic view of the ancient Newland meander of the Wye seen from Kymins Naval Temple, near Monmouth

must mention that the type of rock also plays its part in forming the walls of the theatre—the Quartz Conglomerate forms the scarp edge at least half of the way round. Many farm buildings below are made of it and so also are the rocks in the river at Bigsweir. This weir is interesting, for it is about here that tides finally peter out. Downstream from this point the water is tidal and the brackish water has formed tidal mudflats. Sea level has been rising gradually all round the coasts of the British Isles in the last 10,000 years, the chief cause being the melting of the polar ice cap. The last Ice Age is over, we hope, or we may be in an interglacial period, and the rising sea level has brought the tides up to

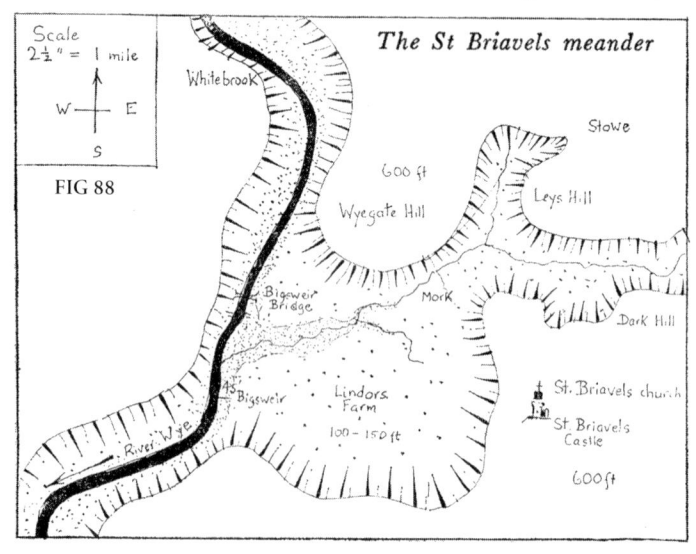

Bigsweir. On the other hand, falling sea level in the last two million years has created the gorges of the Wye and led to the formation of its abandoned meanders.

The Wye valley from Redbrook southwards to Tintern Abbey is a gorge some six miles in length, entrenched into a plateau of Lower Devonian rocks. The block diagram, Figure 91, explains why the scenery is more or less the same, as it is a typical section in which the steep slopes on both sides of the valley are due to the nearly horizontal bands of massive sandstone in the Brownstone series, with the Quartz Conglomerate cropping out high up on the valley side and appearing as crags to enhance the grandeur of the scenery. Figure 91 also shows how the strata dip gradually to the east as it is the western limb of the Dean synclinal basin, the general structure of which was explained in Chapter 3. Part of the Carboniferous Limestone series crops out high up on the 600-foot plateau at Highbury Plain, shown in the block diagram, and southwards it forms an extensive plateau from Stowe and east of St Briavels to Hewelsfield. This area is the most extensive outcrop of the Carboniferous Limestone in the whole of the Dean region and forms a very noticeable feature, easily distinguished as it is mainly given over to grassland and arable land

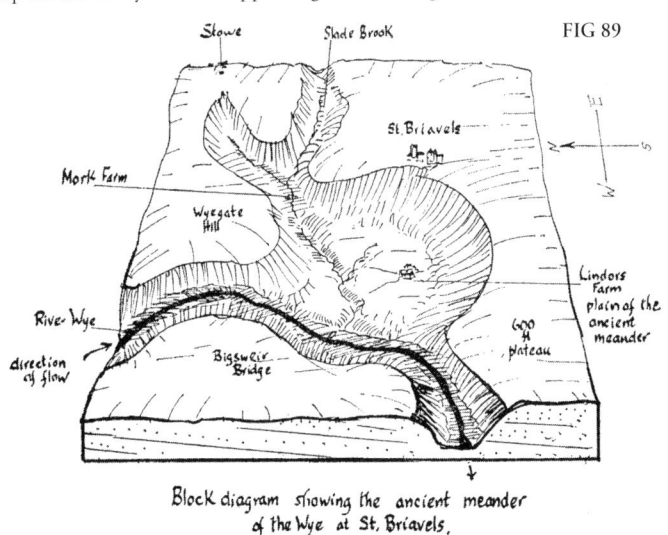

FIG 89

Block diagram showing the ancient meander of the Wye at St. Briavels.

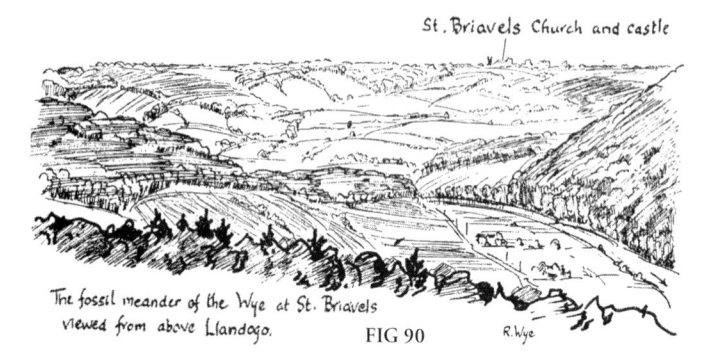

The fossil meander of the Wye at St. Briavels viewed from above Llandogo.

FIG 90

with few forested areas. It is also very conspicuous because of its flat-topped, table-like topography with a constant elevation of 650 feet.

As already pointed out in the Symond's Yat area, the weathering of limestone is mainly by solution, but this is a very slow process and in any case most of the rainfall runs down into the joints, dissolving out the rock below and forming underground rivers. In this way limestone plateaux tend to be beautifully preserved in the form of wide, extensive, table-land country. With the thin soils developed on them, they are better suited to grassland than trees and make quite a contrast on both sides of the valley where the Brownstones are

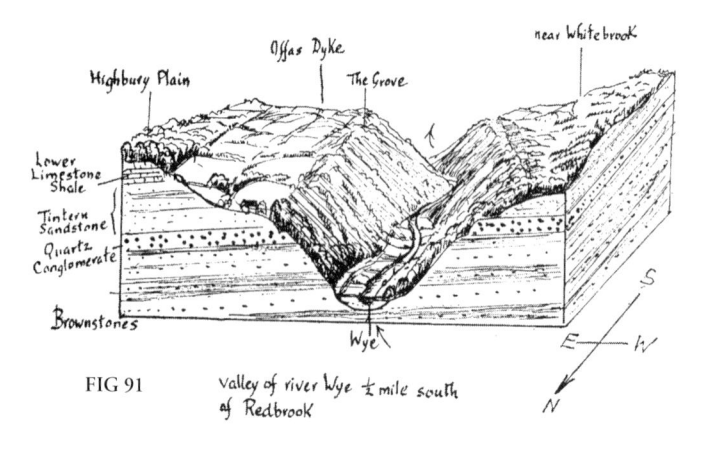

FIG 91 Valley of river Wye ¼ mile south of Redbrook

thickly forested. Good views of this limestone plateau are obtained from the hills around Clearwell and such areas come out very well on aerial photographs. Not all sandstone country is forested, and in the area between Penalt and Trelleck on the western side of the Wye gorge there are large areas of good farmland developed on the soils derived from the Tintern Sandstone group which are softer and not so pebbly as the sandstones of the Lower Devonian.

A visit should be made to Trelleck to see the famous Harold Stones which are about a quarter of a mile from the village. These upright stones, shown in Figure 92,

The Harold Stones at Trelleck. Blocks of pebbly sandstone (Brownstones) used for a Long Barrow Mound - about 2500 B.C. Rain erosion along bedding planes.

FIG 92

are of a pebbly sandstone, possibly from the Brownstones, and it is believed that they formed part of an earthwork known as a long barrow, in which these upright stones were part of a covered cairn. The Neolithic people who built these tombs left behind similar long barrows in the Cotswolds in the Quartz Conglomerate, probably the only group in the whole region—for what quarry worker in his senses would want to work at a tough rock like this? But here there are exceptional conditions, for this rock, which is more resistant than any other in the entire region, is so soft that it can be dug out with a shovel as a gravel and used for making concrete! According to the experts, it has here been exposed to such excessive weathering that the siliceous matrix has dissolved out, though this does not explain why that has occurred here and nowhere else. The problem

FIG 93

Exposure of the Quartz Conglomerate in old quarries West of Trelleck Common. The rock is so weathered that it can be dug out with a spade for gravel

awaits further field work. Gemstone seekers please note that, instead of desperately trying to prise out the jasper pebbles in the Buckstone or Suckstone, just go to these gravel outcrops where you can pick up loose specimens. Figure 93 shows one of these disused quarries, near Trelleck.

About two and a half miles north of Tintern Abbey there is a more spectacular section of the gorge, where the Quartz Conglomerate towers up high above the river, and the sketch, Figure 94, shows how steep are the valley sides compared with those between Redbrook and Bigsweir. Here, too, canoeists must guard against their craft being gashed on the fallen blocks in the river. The writer has checked the type of rock by asking a salmon fisher to exchange his rod for a geologist's hammer in order to extract a sample from the waters of the Wye.

Cleddon Shoots is a well-known tourists' rendezvous near here, where a cascade formed by a river tumbles over the Quartz Conglomerate. The walk is up through a very steep ravine with numerous fallen blocks, but one must wait for a rainy period for Cleddon Shoots to put on a show. When followed up on to the plateau top, the same stream flows across a swampy area of peat bog 750 feet above the river Wye. The sketch, Figure 95, which has been drawn just outside the village of Llandogo, shows what a sight it would be if we had monsoon rains. Very slowly the waterfall is being eroded upstream and in a few hundred thousand years time there will probably be another gorge formed by the recession of the waterfall, for gorges can be formed in other ways than by the process of a falling sea level.

Before we come to the Tintern Abbey area, there is a rapid change of scene on the left bank of the river at Brockweir, where there is another kind of natural amphitheatre known as Hewelsfield Common. Here the steep walls of the Wye gorge give way to a more subdued relief, so that we have numerous small cottages perched all over the hills overlooking the valley. This more open section of the Wye gorge is due to the presence of numerous faults in the Upper Devonian rocks (Tintern Sandstone group), so that the outcrop of these softer strata occurs over a wider area resulting in fewer sharper features of relief and more arable land. Incidentally, if parking a car near the small bridge at Brockweir, remember that, in

Steep scarp of Quartz Conglomerate at Llandogo. Notice fallen blocks in the river

FIG 94

FIG 95 — Cleddon Shoots at Llandogo (Quartz Conglomerate scarp; Cleddon Shoots)

times of spring tides, about twice a month, the water may rise ten feet or more very rapidly. So park well above the river, if possible.

Tintern Abbey is built of local stone, including both Devonian and Carboniferous, and, as one would expect, it is mainly of Tintern Sandstone for there are many old quarries in this rock which the monks must have used. One such quarry is in the core of a meander just north of the abbey and as most of the building is in the Devonian sandstones we can get a true notion of the colour of the rock in the afternoon sun; it is undoubtedly reddish brown but not so red as when freshly quarried. This is because the red haematite mineral which colours the sandstone begins to change to the yellow brown mineral, limonite, on weathering. The monks quarried stone and they also delved for iron ore, as the place name of 'Old Furnace' in a nearby valley indicates. Just south of Chapel Hill at Minepit Wood there are also some old 'scowles' areas where iron has been mined. These are the only remaining evidence of iron mining on the western side of the Wye; all the other 'scowles' are east of the river.

Chapter 13

The Wye Valley: Tintern to Chepstow

ABOUT a mile south of Tintern Abbey, the river Wye enters limestone country once more. The river leaves the limestones of the Seven Sisters Rocks above Monmouth and for the next fifteen miles flows through Old Red Sandstones. A fine scarp of the Carboniferous Limestone can be seen from the river at the Devil's Pulpit, while on the opposite bank are the 700 foot-high cliffs of the Lower Dolomite, known as Black Cliff. As the rocks are dipping eastwards across the valley, as remarked in other stretches of the Wye valley, there is a tendency for a strong scarp to form on one side of the valley only. (See Figure 94.) At Black Cliff there has been the largest landslide in the whole region, huge masses of the Dolomite having slipped down from the 700 foot-high scarp. It is thickly forested but there is access from the main road, A466, about half a mile south of Tintern Abbey. The recommended walk is to follow Offa's Dyke from the Devil's Pulpit, then southwards to Ban-y-gor Rocks. It is rather curious that once the Wye re-enters the limestone country the big wide meanders are preserved and there are no signs of any abandoned ones. This may have something to do with what has been quoted in a previous chapter, that the slow weathering of limestones by solution tends to preserve land forms in this rock for longer periods than those in sandstones. These limestones are more resistant to erosion than the Old Red Sandstone.

We have four large meanders here: Liveoaks, Lancaut, Piercfield and Chepstow, and these are shown on the map, Figure 96. King Offa allowed the Welsh the whole of the Lancaut meander, his eighth-century rampart stretches across the neck of the meander between Ban-y-gor Rocks and Wintour's Leap.

The whole of this region from Black Cliff down to Chepstow is excellent for the study of the Carboniferous Limestone series, of which there are excellent exposures in numerous cliffs and quarries. Quarrying is becoming a major industry here, not only because the rocks crop out in numerous places but because transport facilities for shifting rock to nearby motorways under construction are excellent. Most of the quarries are highly mechanised and this has resulted in the exposure of large cliff faces of white limestone that are now really marking the landscape.

It is perhaps necessary at this stage to explain the origin of many kinds of limestones found in the Lower Carboniferous series in this

FIG 96

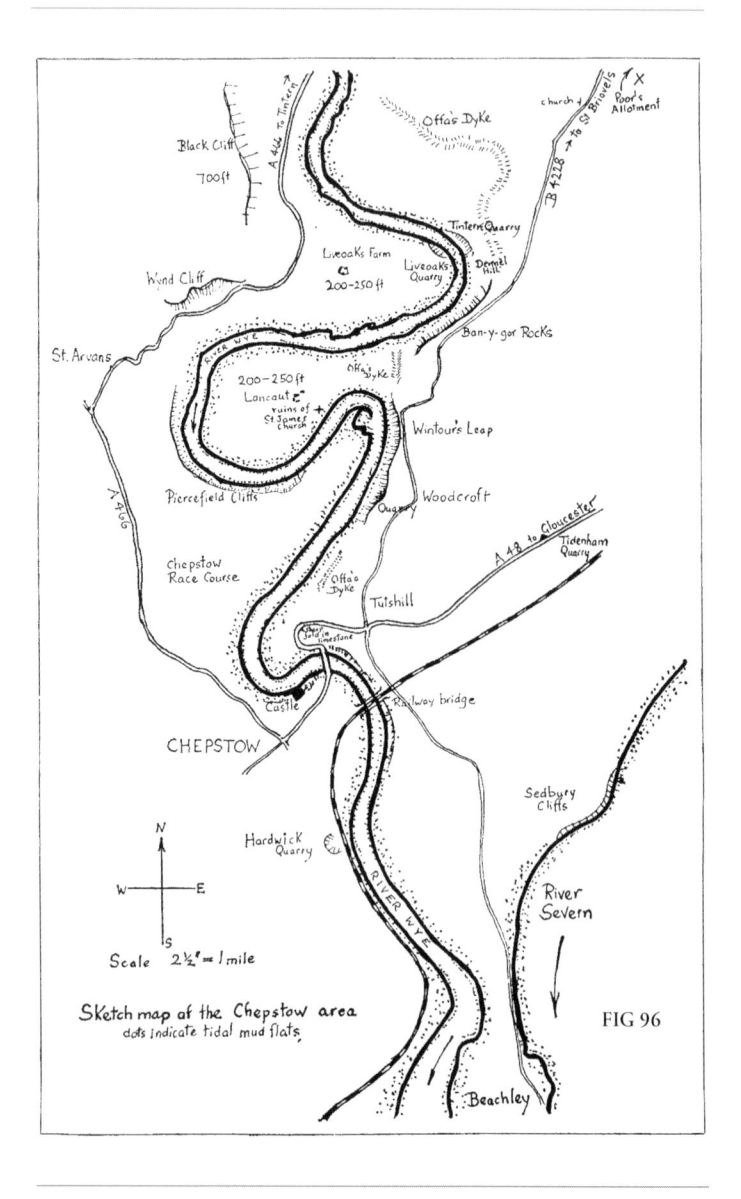

Sketch map of the Chepstow area
dots indicate tidal mud flats.

area. Calcium carbonate deposited in the form of shells and other organic structures can form thick deposits on the sea floor, and if there is one dominant type of fossil present, such as crinoids, the consolidated rock will be termed crinoidal limestone. This is very common in the Lower Limestone Shale and a fair exposure of crinoidal limestone may be seen close to the Devil's Pulpit. Many calcareous algae (microscopic plants) merely cause precipitation of calcium carbonate from the surrounding film of sea water, as they extract from it the carbon dioxide needed in photosynthesis. This precipitate settles over organic material on the sea floor and forms a spongy deposit of fine particles which become a lime mud. When this consolidates into a rock, a process termed 'lithification', the result is a limestone which, at first glance, is without fossils. However, we can often see concentric structures which record the positions of successive growths of algae. This is common in the Whitehead Limestone and a good place to collect specimens is at Piercefield Cliffs (see map, Figure 96). Here one can find concentrically-ringed nodules, up to two inches across, of the giant alga called *Garwoodia gregaria*.

When one enters these large quarries in the Chepstow area a quarryman may remark, 'No fossils here, mate, and I've been here for five years.' In fact, it is more a matter of seeing only what you know. There are, of course, non-fossiliferous limestones that have been formed chemically, but there is a limit to the solubility of calcium carbonate in sea water and the important factor affecting this is the CO_2 (carbon dioxide) content of the water. This varies with the temperature and the number of plants, such as algae, living in the sea water. The algae will reduce the amount of CO_2 in the water and cause precipitation of $CaCO_3$ (calcium carbonate). In this way a chemical limestone of organic origin is formed, which we would expect to be rather unfossiliferous.

In this area there are two very large and busy quarries in the Lower Dolomite, one at Liveoaks, called Livox Quarry, and the other in the suburbs of Chepstow at Hardwick. The origin of dolomite is still uncertain. There are two theories. The first one, known as the primary precipitation theory, is that it was precipitated direct from seawater. The second, and perhaps the better theory is that previously existing calcium carbonate deposits were changed to dolomite on the sea floor or after slight burial, and this is called the 'penecontemporaneous replacement theory'. Dolomite rock is found in rocks of different geological ages, but in Dean it is always found with ordinary

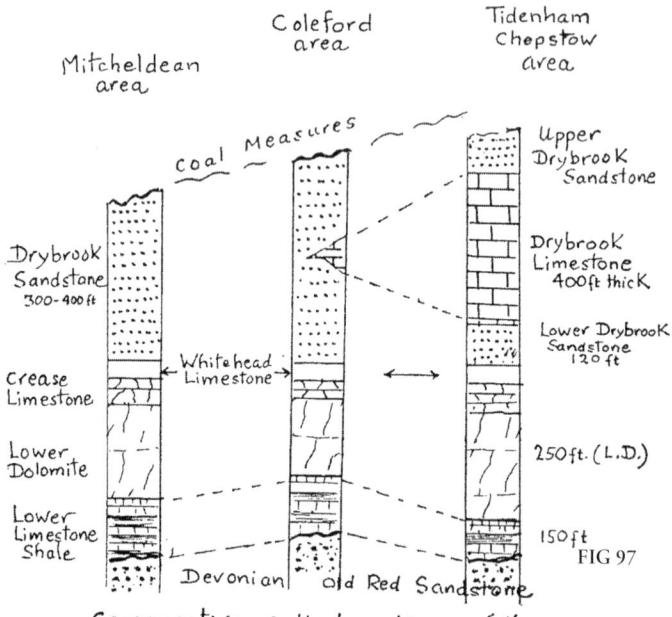

Geology Explained in the Forest of Dean and Wye Valley

Comparative vertical sections of the Lower Carboniferous Limestone Series in 3 areas, east, central and west Dean.

FIG 97

Mitcheldean area — Drybrook Sandstone 300-400 ft; Crease Limestone; Lower Dolomite; Lower Limestone Shale; Devonian.

Coleford area — Coal Measures; Whitehead Limestone; Old Red Sandstone.

Tidenham Chepstow area — Upper Drybrook Sandstone; Drybrook Limestone 400 ft thick; Lower Drybrook Sandstone 120 ft; 250 ft. (L.D.); 150 ft.

limestones, and it is here apparently stratigraphically controlled, ie, layers of dolomite are succeeded and preceded by limestone strata, the Crease Limestone above and the Lower Limestone Shale below. The best display of all is in Hardwick Quarry where its massive nature and pinkish-grey colour contrasts with the thinly-bedded white limestone above. (See Figure 105.) Most of the dolomites in the world are of this 'stratigraphical' type, but it is strange that only in a few places are dolomites forming today, so that this is a case where the present fails as a key to the past.

However, borings made in some Pacific coral reefs reveal that, deeper down, the limestone coral rock has been converted into dolomite rock after lithification, the change having occurred when the rock was solid. The magnesium atoms are somewhat smaller than those of calcium, but they can exchange with calcium in calcite and this leads to a close packing of the atoms within what was formerly a calcite rock. This explains why dolomite is both a harder and denser rock than limestone. It also helps to explain why fossils are partly destroyed or only the moulds seen in the rock. Dolomite can be compared with writing on a manuscript which has been rubbed out to make room for fresh writing, leaving the old writing still faintly showing. The term 'palimpsest' is used to describe this and this palimpsest feature of dolomite is an argument in favour of the replacement theory. However, masses of dolomite may show no relics of fossils at all.

The diagram. Figure 97, shows comparative vertical sections in the Carboniferous Limestone series in various parts of the Dean region. It shows that the Drybrook Sandstone, which is 400 feet thick in the Mitcheldean area, begins in the Coleford area to have a band of limestone which, in the Chepstow locality, becomes 400 feet thick with sandstone both above and below. It is this limestone which tends to dominate the scenery on the left bank of the Wye between Chepstow and Ban-y-gor rocks. The sections in Figure 97 show that the Lower Dolomite thickens to the south-west of the region, reaching a maximum thickness of 600 feet in the Caerwent syncline, a few miles west of Chepstow.

The reasons for this change can be explained by contemporary earth movements and reference to the 'ancient geography', or palaeogeography of the Carboniferous period. For at this time there was a large land mass stretching from Wales to the Central Midlands known as 'St George's Land', and as this was uplifted by the earth movements, rivers flowing south were speeded up (rejuvenated) and swept down great quantities of sand into a shallow sea that lay in the Dean area.

How do we know that it was a shallow sea? The Whitehead Limestone which underlies the Drybrook Sandstone indicates shallow water conditions with algal calcite mudstones which are best displayed in Scully Grove near Mitcheldean and in Tintern Quarry on the left bank of the Wye opposite Liveoaks farm. It is believed that earth movements generating these conditions occurred along the Lower Severn and Bath Axes. (See Chapter 3, on the main structures of the region.) Figure 97 also shows that the strata of the Coal Measures rest on the eroded surface of the Drybrook Sandstone in some places, but the only place in this locality is a quarter of a mile SSE of Chase House at Poor's Allotment, where there is

tidal mud flats — Tintern Quarry opposite Liveoaks farm   FIG 98

evidence of shallow coal workings in two fields close to the St Briavels road, B4228. There are scattered fragments of blue mudstone and coal shale in the top soil, but this is the only place in south-west Dean where Coal Measures are found and it is probably a relic of a much larger area of the Coal Measures that has been eroded, leaving this patchy outcrop on the downthrow side of the St Briavels fault. About a few hundred yards south of Poor's Allotment, at the spot marked 'X' on the sketch map (Figure 96) there is an excellent viewpoint across the Clanna pericline to the Severn and Lydney. The height is 700 feet and blocks of the Drybrook Sandstone are scattered about the site, which is now a National Trust area.

Tintern Quarry is reached by a branch road from B4228 leading from Tidenham Chase to the Wye valley. The view of the quarry shown in Figure 98 is from Ban-y-gor rocks and shows how the Wye gorge becomes much more impressive when its meanders are entrenched in limestones. Tintern Quarry consists of two high cliff faces displaying the Whitehead Limestone, the best exposure of this rock in Dean. The bedding planes are regularly spaced and in places there are bands of calcite mudstone. This looks like a breccia, ie, angular fragments set in a hard mudstone to which the name 'pseudo breccia' is given. It can be made into excellent ornamental stone by taking large lumps to a stone mason who can saw through them. If the flat sawn surface is then painted with polyurethane, very pretty structures become visible, some being concentric patterns which might be due to algal colonies. When the uninitiated look at the 200-foot high cliffs of limestone they often wonder how long it took to deposit these strata. Throughout the Palaeozoic Era which lasted some 400 million years, the average rate of deposition was about one foot in 2,700 years. However, a geologist would not apply this estimate to any section of strata for the simple reason that sedimentation processes vary considerably and sediment is moved about many times on the sea floor before finally settling down. There may be short breaks in deposition, called diastems, and there is no record of this time interval in the strata. However, the junction of the Whitehead Limestone and the Crease Limestone must represent a long interval of time between these two changes in sedimentation, and this junction can be seen in the railway cutting close to the tunnel through Dennel Hill. It is interesting to note that the quarry company bought the disused railway line and now use it for taking the stone to the main line at Tidenham.

On the opposite side of the river to Tintern Quarry is Liveoaks (Livox) Quarry, where the extensive cliffs show sixty feet of the blue-grey Lower Dolomite. The dip here is at 10 degrees to the east, so that at Tintern Quarry, opposite, the dolomite is well below the quarry floor. But here the cliff top has just reached the base of the Lower Drybrook Sandstone, so that the only economic way to continue operations is by excavating down to reach the Lower Dolomite.

Wynd Cliff is a well-known beauty spot and the approach should be made by crossing the Wye either at Chepstow or Tintern and following the A466 road. The viewpoint is from the top of the cliffs of Lower Dolomite, 750 feet above the river, and the sketch, Figure 99, shows that the view takes in most of the meander, the core of which reveals rather a low uniform

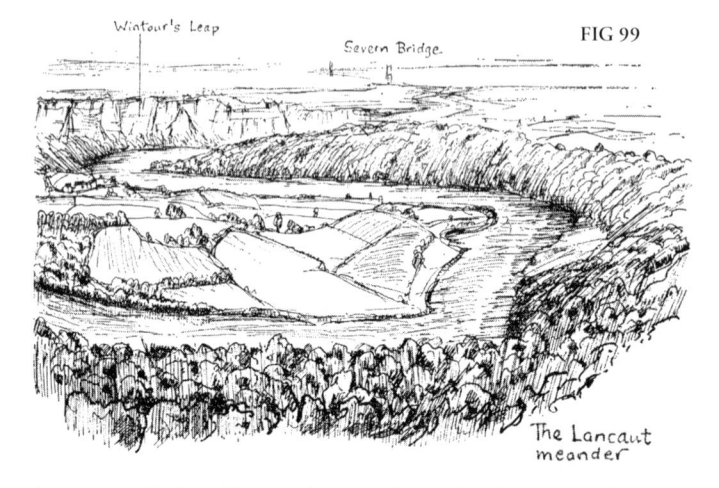

Figure 99 — Wintour's Leap, Severn Bridge, The Lancaut meander

plateau at 250 feet. This marks a more recent stage in the history of the Wye and it can be matched with the Liveoaks plain, which is at the same height (see map, Figure 96). It points to the fact that sea level did not fall continuously and that there were intermittent pauses during which these plains or river terraces were formed.

The best view of the Liveoaks meander is from Ban-y-gor rocks, to which there is access close to the St Briavels road. The cliffs here consist of 200 feet of Drybrook Limestone which now begins to crop out all along this bank of the Wye to near Chepstow and forms high towering cliffs. Wintour's Leap ranks with Wynd Cliff as one of the outstanding beauty spots for Chepstow visitors. It is named after a Cavalier, General Winter, who is supposed to have leapt over this cliff in the Civil War. The sketches. Figures 100 and 101, show the 300-feet high cliffs of Drybrook Limestone, which is here oolitic. Although the cliffs are inaccessible, the strata show good bedding planes and strong vertical joints which provide scope for many rock-climbing clubs whose members, on some busy weekends, have literally to queue up for the ascent.

The diagram, Figure 102, explains why there are high cliffs on one side of the river here, and in most cases they are naturally formed by blocks slipping away from the vertical joints. A footpath along the clifftop leads to the old quarry at Woodcroft, from which

FIG 100

Wintour's Leap

large slabs of stone were used in the construction of Avonmouth Docks. This is also the best place to study the Drybrook Limestone and on the bedding planes of tumbled blocks can be seen masses of the coral, *Lithostrotion martini*, with the brachiopods, *Productus* and *Composite*. This is the typical brachiopod-coral assemblage, a feature of many Palaeozoic limestones. Another footpath leads down to the Wye and passes small cliffs of the Lower Drybrook Sandstone, here only 100 feet thick, which crop out 30 feet above the river.

The tidal mud-flats are quite extensive here because there is often a 20-foot rise with high tide. The actual shore line given on a map is always the high-water mark above mean tides. In the past ten years, tidal scours have eaten out chunks of meadow, nearly all to a crescent shape, and one of these can be seen by Piercefield Cliffs opposite Wintour's Leap.

Figure 103 shows that Chepstow Castle is in an almost impregnable position from the river side. It is built on crags of the Crease Limestone that rise vertically from the saltwater mud-flats, and a walk round the ditch surrounding the curtain walls of the castle will reveal plenty of exposures for those wishing to study this type of rock. From the main road bridge at Chepstow, magnificent examples of the folding

Wintour's Leap from the mud banks of the Wye

FIG 101

can be seen in the Drybrook Limestone, the folds extending all along the cliffs down to the railway bridge. The whole range of folds can be studied from the public pleasure gardens bordering the river. A very sharp fold can be seen by the main road 200 yards north of Chepstow road bridge (see map, Figure 96). Figure 104 shows this sharp anticline, which is interesting because it reveals an example of drag folds which form when a strong bed slides past a weaker one, generating small crumple' folds in the latter. Similar sharp folds with drag folds

FIG 102

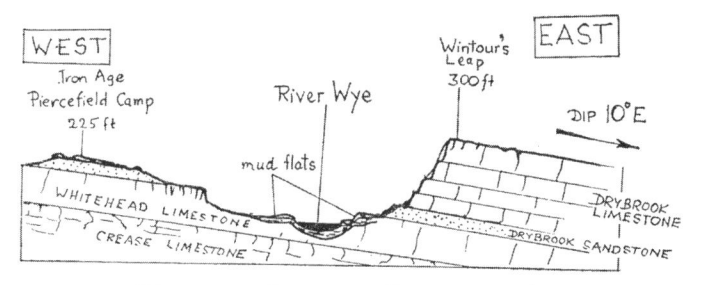

Diagram explaining why there are much higher limestone cliffs on one bank of the Wye than the other. Notice how the Iron Age tribes chose an outcrop of sandstone (Drybrook) as drier ground for their settlement

can be seen along a forest road in Grove Wood, two miles north of Lydbrook, but these are developed in the Lower Limes shale.

If one observes the receding tide from Chepstow Bridge it is possible to see in miniature what has happened to the Wye. Tiny streams flow down the steep mud banks, each rivulet having many 'mini-meanders'. These meanders measure only a few inches across but they are quite regular and as the tide falls the erosive power of these tiny streams is speeded up, so that the meanders become incised into the soft mud

Chepstow Castle on the Crease Limestone

FIG 103

in the space of a few hours—well illustrating, in miniature, what the Wye took a million years or more to accomplish.

Finally, one must go to Hardwick Quarry which lies close to the railway south of Chepstow town. Figure 105 shows the crag which represents the finest exposure for comparing the Lower Dolomite with the Crease Limestone. Here both types of rock are quarried and the writer has been assured by the manager that this fine crag will be preserved.

We have now examined the scenery of the Wye valley from Ross down to the estuary at Chepstow, and it clearly shows that, throughout, the river flows independently of the controls of structural geology. It is nevertheless true to state that there are many variations in valley slopes due to variations in rock type, as demonstrated by the cliffs of limestone and Quartz Conglomerate. The manner in which the Wye ignores the structures of the rocks can only be explained in terms of its recent history. There is evidence of at least three stages of erosion in this section of the river. First, the highest plateau of all, of which today only a few small remnants

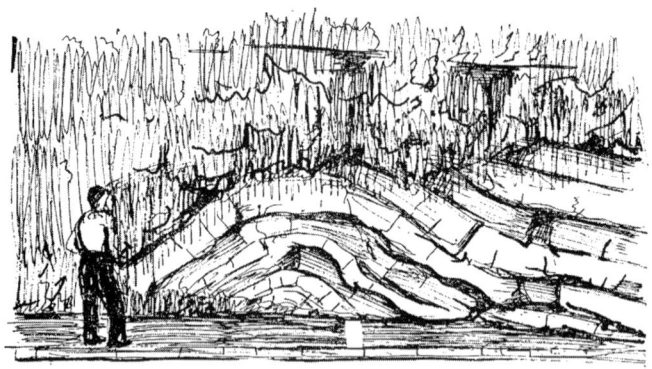

Small anticline in the Whitehead limestone visible from the main road 200 yds north of Chepstow bridge

FIG 104

structure section of a symmetrical fold showing relation of drag folds to bedding planes

exist; the 900-foot plateau as shown on Trelleck Common, the Buckstone and Ruardean Hill. Secondly, the 500-foot stage, which is well shown on Tidenham Chase and many other places. Thirdly, the 200- to 250-foot stage so well shown on the Liveoaks and Lancaut meander cores. The general term of superimposed drainage is given to this kind of river system.

How has all this happened? Many geologists believe that the successive stages can be correlated with periodic withdrawals of the sea that have occurred during the last two million years. But the latest episode of all was probably during the last three thousand years when the rising level of the sea, due to the melting ice caps flooding the lower Wye and Severn, caused the tides to extend up the Wye to Bigsweir, a rise that has affected the lower courses of all rivers in the British Isles and north-west Europe.

FIG 105 — Hardwick Quarry, Chepstow (Crease Limestone; Lower Dolomite)

Chapter 14

The Scowles

THERE is only one place by the name of Scowles in the whole of the region; a small hamlet about half a mile west of Coleford; but 'scowles' is the local term for any area where there are ancient shallow workings for iron ore. It is believed by some that the name is derived from an old Welsh word meaning recess or hollow, while another idea is that the word is of modern origin meaning rubbish or debris. However, many of these places date from the Middle Ages, and some even go back to the Roman period. In this chapter, most of the scowles areas will be dealt with, but the origin of the iron will be left to the following chapter.

The visitor to Newland Church should see the brass effigy to a Forest of Dean miner which dates from the fifteenth century and shows the worker carrying a mattock implement in his hand, a wooden hod strapped to his shoulder and in his mouth a stick to which is attached a piece of clay to hold a candle. It is unusual to find an effigy of a 'common worker' among the knights and ladies of the church, and this one is probably unique in Britain. The last iron mines here closed down during the Second World War, but for centuries before that Dean ore was much in demand because of its high quality, and even in Edward the Confessor's time royalty required iron for rods, bolts and chains for the king's ships. It is recorded that in 1282 sixty forges were at work, most of them being in eastern Dean, whereas most of the iron mines were located on the Wye side of Dean for reasons which will be explained in the next chapter.

The best known scowles in the area, commonly called the Devil's Chapel, is half a mile south of Bream, adjacent to and easily accessible from the B4231 road from Lydney. It is open to the public and, as may be seen in the sketch. Figure 106, showing the approach through the woods, the upturned edges of the Crease Limestone almost direct the curious to explore further and follow the dip downwards. It is quite likely that in pre-Roman times the Iron Age tribes worked the ore and traded it with the Romans. Once a vein was discovered it was followed as 'the lead', which might bring the miner to a large pocket of iron occupying an underground hollow which was termed a 'churn'. At first, of course, the workings were very shallow and no deep shafts were drilled until about 1830. Here is a quotation from the famous book. Iron Making in the Olden Times, by the Rev H. G. Nicholls, originally

Scowles. Devil's Chapel   FIG 106

published in 1866 and reprinted by David and Charles in 1965.

There are, deep in the earth, vast caverns scooped out by men's hands, and large as the aisles of churches; and on its surface are extensive labyrinths worked among the rocks and now long since overgrown with woods, which whosoever traces them must see with astonishment, and incline to think them to have been the work of armies rather than of private labourers. They certainly were the toil of many centuries, and this perhaps before they thought of searching in the bowels of the earth for their ore, whither, however, they at length naturally pursued the veins, as they found them to be exhausted near the surface.

Written in 1780 by a Mr Wyrrall

After plunging down into one of the hollows the explorer can follow the 'lead' along a line of chasms and labyrinths and return from the other end by way of a parallel line of small canyons. He is unlikely to get lost if he observes the general dip of the limestone which is 15 degrees NW. The limestone walls are riddled with gaping joints, some of which have been widened to allow passage through into the next 'chapel'. There is not just one Devil's Chapel but many into which he can pry. He will observe that many of the rock pinnacles and open joints show rounded or semicircular structures resembling chimneys, which look as if they had been dissolved out by some chemical process or were funnels which have been filled with iron ore. The sketch Figure 107 shows part of such a chimney in the

The Scowles. Devil's Chapel   FIG 107

central stack of limestone.

In wandering in these labyrinths one comes often to semi-circular 'corners' at the bottom of the chimneys, each providing the Devil with a natural apse for his chapel. Sometimes the approach is made through a hole in a joint which is either man-made or just caused by solution. Here and there can be seen thin crusts of iron ore and everywhere the rock is stained red with it. The rock is mostly dolomite and the ore mineral is haematite. It is remarkable to see how in all the scowles the yew tree loves to twine its roots round the haematite-impregnated rock, and this might be an interesting subject for botanical investigation. In all scowles the dominant trees are yew, beech, ash, elm and hazel, the dense vegetation adding gloom to the bizarre rock forms and creating an eerie place ideal for the practice of witchcraft.

Figure 108 shows how the old miners followed a lead of ore along the bedding planes of the rather massive rock, while here and there deviations were made to dig out ore. In some places these branches or 'leads' proceed further into wide open churns underground. The rock is strongly jointed and Figure 109 shows how sometimes the 'chimneys' collapse and block up ancient entrances to the chums. It was while removing such stones in 1854 that men found a pile of Roman silver coins, a discovery which suggests that some of the scowles probably date back to the second century AD. It is difficult to imagine how the old miners with their simple mattocks and oak shovels removed all this rock, but we must remember that we are looking at workings where excavations went on for 2,000 years.

The next area of scowles, known as the Devil's Ditch, is found in Old Park Wood just south of the Devil's

FIG 108

The Scowles. Devils Chapel

Chapel. This is a naturally-formed, long, gaping joint but opened up by shallow workings. It is in the Lower Dolomite and not the Crease Limestone and if we follow the Ditch it leads to the site of the villa in Lydney Park where, according to Sir Mortimer Wheeler, we have true evidence that the Romans worked the ore on their estate. A return journey can be made by following the Park Brook, a southward-flowing stream which has cut a remarkable gorge into the Lower Dolomite at Lodge Farm. This is a good example of a 'superimposed river', for it flows right across the different strata in its course through Dean. It is probable that the iron ore from both the Devil's Ditch and Devil's Chapel went to the Sir John Wintour iron works which was destroyed during

The Scowles. Devils Chapel

FIG 109

The Scowles near Clearwell   Deanpool Farm   FIG 110

the Civil War, about 1640.

A small scowles at Bream Tufts, a few hundred yards north of the Miner's Arms in Bream, may be entered from the old quarry in the Lower Dolomite which is visible from the road leading to deal-well. Proceeding northwards, constantly following the Crease Limestone which can be recognised by open grassland usually found on this type of rock, it is easy to see areas of scowles for they are heavily wooded and a rather sinuous belt of woods denotes an outcrop of the Crease Limestone.

At Noxon Park, which can be reached by taking the B4231 road to Clearwell and turning off at the well known Noxon Pond near Noxon Farm, a scowles area with a large man-made cave can be seen. In recent years this has been more difficult of access as it

Scowles near Clearwell, Deanpool Farm   FIG 111

is gradually filling up with water but it was once an exciting place to explore. Following the track to Clements Tump, one passes many old iron workings in a steep gorge in the Lower Dolomite, which quite suddenly opens into the Coal Measures of the Dean basin.

Few people know of the scowles at Deanpool Farm in the limestone ridge overlooking the pretty village of Clearwell. Here there are two main ore joints which have been opened out by shallow workings. Figure 110 shows a deep, natural, gaping joint used by the miners when seeking ore, while Figure 111 depicts a chimney type of canyon and is a good example of solution cavities which formerly contained pockets of iron ore. This area is just as spectacular as the Devil's Chapel but, as it is privately owned, permission to enter must be obtained. Having gained admission, visitors should be very careful to close gates for in summer cattle often like to go into the scowles to escape from flies. In winter, the animals find such places too draughty but recently, during severe weather when snow covered the ground, several hungry cattle seeking food in the scowles nibbled at yew branches and were poisoned. Such a serious loss to the owner may be avoided if visitors exercise due consideration and care.

Not far from Deanpool, in Clearwell Meend, is the famous British Mine, the resort of many cavers and potholers. About fifty yards from the steps leading down to the entrance there is a spacious underground chamber large enough to hold a hundred people. A visitor should not enter alone and he should carry a good torch to enable him to see the fine examples of stalactites and crystal formations of calcite, dolomite and haematite. These workings extend for a considerable distance underground but no attempt should be made to explore them without first consulting the Forest of Dean Caving Society which has made accurate maps of many of these old iron workings and underground levels. This one at Clearwell is part of the Old Ham Mine, although on some maps it is marked as 'British Mine'. Every free miner has the right to mine an area known as a gale and the maps held by the society show the extent of each gale. This mine is so frequently visited that it may perhaps become necessary to put a gate at the entrance to prevent spoliation of the interior which is such an ideal and safe place in which to study limestone formations. On the opposite side of the road to Ham Mine there is the air shaft of an old mine and this leads down to extensive underground workings that take about three hours to explore. However, this is not for the ordinary visitor and an experienced caver should be enlisted as a guide.

A few hundred yards north is Lambsquay Wood scowles, the only place in Dean where the former owner has transformed his ancient scowles into a landscape garden with little bridges, ladders and crazy paths. Unfortunately, vandals soon wrecked the little park and one must now get permission to enter from Lower Perrygrove Farm.

The tiny village of Scowles, situated half a mile west of Coleford on the road from Crossways to Redbrook, is an interesting example of a typical German 'strassendorf', or one-street village consisting of old miners' cottages built alongside the usual linear pattern of scowles areas. This area, which is also privately owned, is less spectacular than the Deanpool Farm or Devil's Chapel scowles but if the tour is extended to the very large active quarry in the Lower Dolomite at Whitecliff, one can see the massive rock dipping at 15 degrees eastwards into the Dean basin.

Our list of the iron workings in

[FIG 112] Drummer Boy Stone (Quartz Conglomerate) Blackpool Bridge — smelted iron

Sign: DRUMMER BOY STONE / ARTIFICIAL HOLLOW / CONTAINS SMELTED IRON / ORIGIN UNKNOWN

West Dean can now be completed with just a mention of small scowles areas near Hangerberry in the Lydbrook valley, and some in Blakes wood, south of Staunton.

In northern Dean, one would expect to find old iron workings in the Symond's Yat area and this has already been mentioned in connection with the Yat Rock. Some local historians believe that King Arthur's Cave is really an old iron mine but this is not sound geological reasoning. It is more likely that Merlin's Cave, which is in the Crease Limestone, is a genuine habitation of ancient Man but has been developed much later by iron-ore seekers. A very interesting labyrinth of scowles is by Merlin's Cave in the cliffs above Cinder Island, close to Symond's Yat. As already mentioned, the only old iron workings west of the river Wye are to be found in Minepit Wood, about a quarter of a mile north of Wynd Cliff, and it is quite likely that in the Middle Ages the ore from there was sent to the Tintern Abbey charcoal furnace.

We now come to the workings in East Dean, the oldest of which are perhaps in Lining Wood on the Mitcheldean side of Wigpool Common. There are records of caves and pits here but little can be seen today except a few scowles by the 'Yankee Cinema' mentioned in an earlier chapter. The famous Wigpool Mine is still open at the top and goes down 530 feet through Coal Measures to reach the Crease Limestone. In 1921, the Bailey Level was driven in to drain this mine of water and this revived the story of 'gold mining in Dean'. On this eastern side of Dean, from Wigpool south to Soudley, the strata are highly inclined necessitating deep shafts to reach the ore, so that there are few shallow workings of the scowles type here. A place called the Delves on Wigpool Common is a small scowles which tradition maintains is of Roman origin. Many archaeologists believe that a Roman road went from Lydney to Mitcheldean via Blackpool Bridge, Soudley, Littledean and Abenhall, and it seems possible that the Roman settlement of Ariconium may have had some connection with iron mining which was already established here before the Romans came.

On Plump Hill, close to the active quarry in the Drybrook Sandstone, there is the shaft of the Westbury Brook Mine, which was opened in 1837. In this area, and southwards as far as Littledean, iron ore is found in the Drybrook Sandstone which crops out along the hill crest from Mitcheldean to Ruspidge. Many small scowles occur along this stratum and there are some interesting examples in Edgehills Plantation of development with deep holes rather than workings along gaping joints. Many of these holes have had to be fenced in for the sake of animals belonging to foresters, who still exercise common grazing rights. Mention has already been made in a previous chapter of the large dump of waste rock from the St Annals mine shaft which is 657 feet deep. This is close to the Forester's Arms on Littledean Hill, and if we follow the ridge southwards we come to the last area of scowles above Ruspidge, where there are the important shafts of Shakemantle and Buckshaft. Between 1840 and 1900, about one and a half million tons of ore came from Shakemantle Mine and this led to a great revival of iron-making in the mid-nineteenth century in the Cinderford region.

In south-eastern Dean, in an

FIG 113

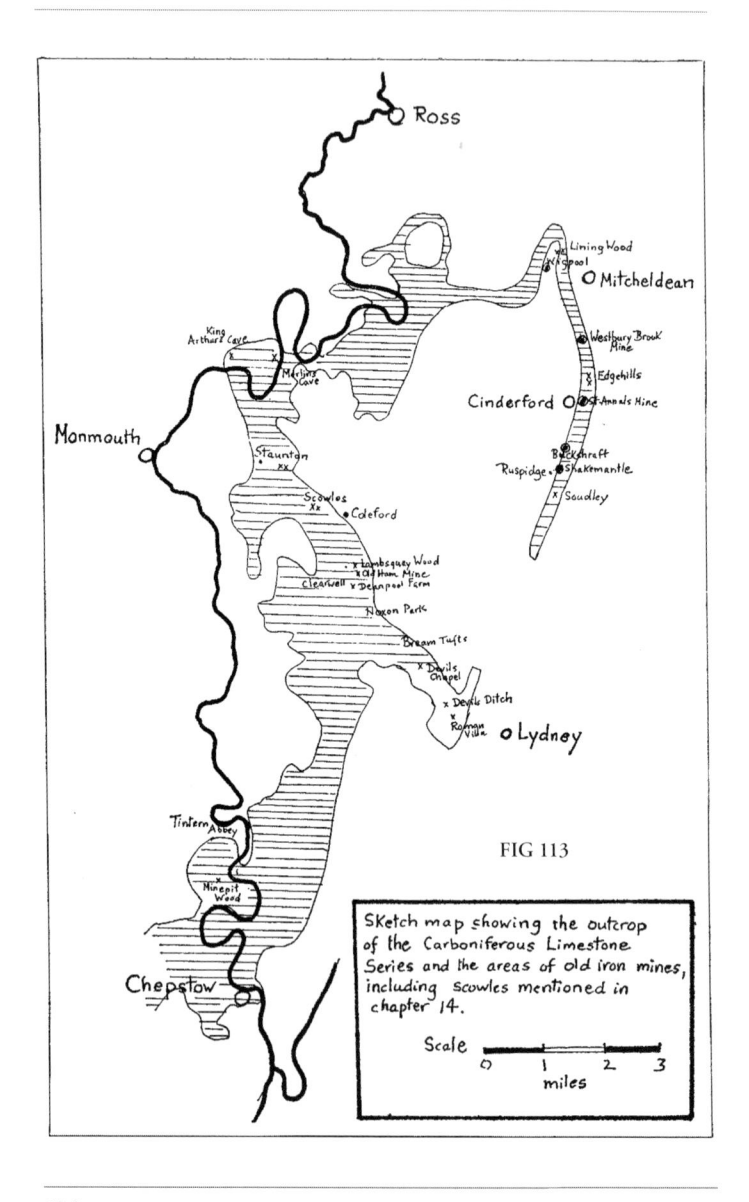

Sketch map showing the outcrop of the Carboniferous Limestone Series and the areas of old iron mines, including scowles mentioned in chapter 14.

Scale 0 1 2 3 miles

area stretching from Soudley to Fiaxley, there are remains of many old iron works. Some, like the one at Soudley, date back to 1565, and there is a record of the monks of Flaxley as early as 1154. There is also a record of oak timber from Dean being used in the building of the bridge over the Severn at Gloucester in 1265. Timber was also required for shipbuilding and, as the centuries passed, demands of this kind conflicted with the interests of iron miners who needed timber to make charcoal for smelting and so led to a decline in the iron industry. The revival came in 1795 when the manufacture of iron was resumed in the Forest with the aid of pit coke from coal at Cinderford. Deep shafts were driven into the Crease Limestone and Drybrook Sandstone and even today the cinders from these prolific iron works can be seen scattered in fields around Cinderford and Parkend, while artificial ponds created at Cannop and Soudley to provide power for the forges now add to the scenic attractions of the area.

Now it is all finished and as ramblers follow the forest paths they catch an occasional gleam of iron slag among the ancient cinders. It is reassuring to note that a proposal in 1955 to dump radio-active waste into the old mines was abandoned. Let us hope that the Forest of Dean Caving Society will strive to preserve the good areas and save them from becoming foul-smelling rubbish dumps.

Visitors to the Forest are reminded of the importance of this area in the Middle Ages by the Drummer Boy Stone (Figure 112). Its origin is unknown but the old iron miners certainly knew that the Quartz Conglomerate was the most suitable rock for making moulds into which to pour molten iron. The sketch map, Figure 113, locates the places mentioned in this chapter.

Chapter 15
The Origin of the Iron Ore

SINCE most sedimentary rocks contain iron minerals in varying amounts, it is necessary to explain where the iron has come from in the first place. The original rocks forming the crust of the earth are igneous and contain many iron minerals, mainly in the form of ferro-magnesian silicates (ferrous silicates). The breakdown of these rocks by ordinary weathering processes produces the final end products of sand and clay and material in solution. We can, therefore, expect to find iron minerals in various sedimentary rocks and as the ultimate destination of rock waste is the sea, it is obvious that marine sediments will contain iron. Various iron compounds are soluble in water, and certain groups of bacteria extract oxygen from iron oxides instead of from air or water. These anaerobic bacteria cause precipitation of iron on to the sea floor and this is another way in which iron gets into marine sedimentary rocks.

What, then, is the explanation of the type of sedimentary rocks known as 'Red beds' that are so familiar in the Devonian and Triassic strata? In this part of Britain these are mainly terrestrial deposits and to answer this question we must examine the situation today in certain areas of the world. At the present time, in all regions of the world where the mean annual temperature is over 60° F and the annual rainfall is 40 inches or more, haematite (ferric oxide) is being formed in the residual soils. During the long hot dry season the strongly oxidising conditions produce this ferric oxide. The most favourable oxidising environment is the savannah climate but the exact chemical evolution of such laterite soils is not fully understood. About 270 million years ago, at the end of the Carboniferous period, desert conditions began and during the succeeding Permian period, which lasted some fifty million years, the sandstones and shales of the Coal Measures in the Forest of Dean were subjected to much weathering and erosion, and probably considerable thicknesses of the Coal Measure strata were destroyed. On examining the various sandstones and shales of this series we find a good deal of iron in the form of iron carbonates and iron sulphide (pyrites). In the strongly oxidising environment of the Permian period, residual soils and rock waste rich in iron must have accumulated on the land surface. After rainy seasons, the iron-bearing acid waters descended on to the underlying limestones, which were highly inclined to the Coal

The Origin of the Iron Ore

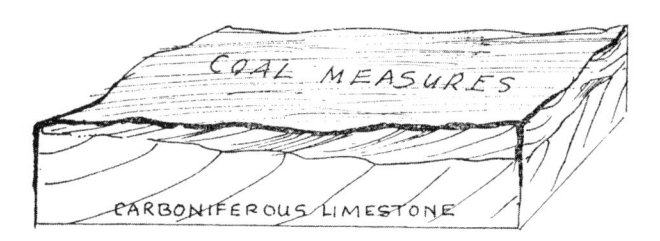

The situation at the end of the Carboniferous period

FIG 114

Measure strata because of the Intra-Carboniferous earth movements as explained in Chapter 3. So the iron solutions entered the joints in the limestones, dissolved out the rock and replaced it with pockets and veins of haematite. As the Crease Limestone is more open textured than other limestone in the series of the Lower Carboniferous, it was more susceptible to replacement. The Lower Dolomite was also penetrated but not so extensively as the joints and bedding planes are not so well developed in this rock. The calcareous bands in parts of the Drybrook Sandstone were also attacked by the descending solutions, so that iron ore is found also in this rock in some places. If one explores any scowles in Dean the fact that iron ore solutions came from above is very evident.

The suggested sequence of events in the Permian period is shown in the diagrams Figures 114 and 115, and

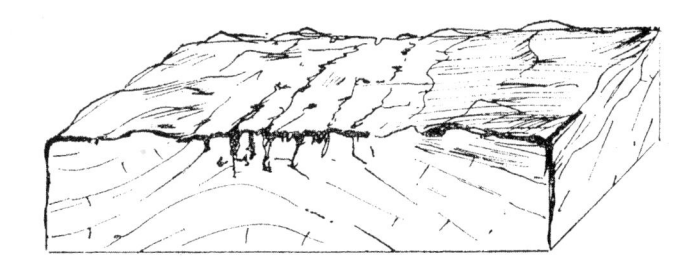

The land surface during the Permian period. An oxidising environment consisting of long hot dry seasons.

FIG 115

here it must be noted that, after the great period of mountain building referred to in Chapter 3 as the Hercynian orogeny, there followed a long period lasting many millions of years during which the Dean area was a land mass. Probably it was never covered by Triassic deposits such as the Keuper Marl, for we find that the Marl is banked up against the Carboniferous Limestones as a scree deposit in the Tidenham area. (See notes on the Tidenham Quarry in a previous chapter.) This interpretation may be open to debate but another suggestion that iron in the limestones came from a covering of Triassic deposits, like the Keuper Marl, is less tenable. To produce such masses of iron ore as we find in scowles would require a greater thickness of Trias than that shown in the surrounding areas to Dean. This theory implies that iron solutions from the Trias descended into the limestones, but it does not explain the absence of iron ore in the limestones of the Tidenham Chase syncline area. It may be that there were iron ore deposits in that area and that subsequent erosion has removed them. However, as stated in a previous chapter, iron ore deposits were found on the west bank of the Wye at Minepit Wood, south of Tintern, near Wynd Cliff.

Throughout the Middle Ages, the iron miners usually searched in

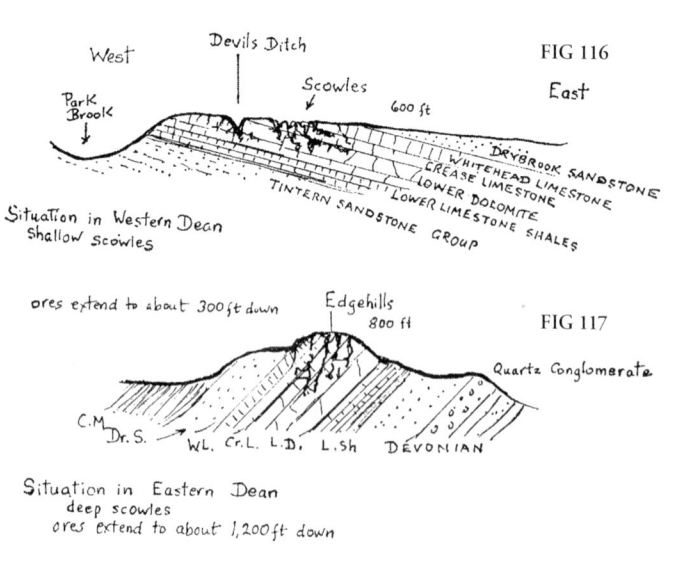

FIG 116

Situation in Western Dean
shallow scowles

FIG 117

Situation in Eastern Dean
deep scowles
ores extend to about 1,200 ft down

The Origin of the Iron Ore

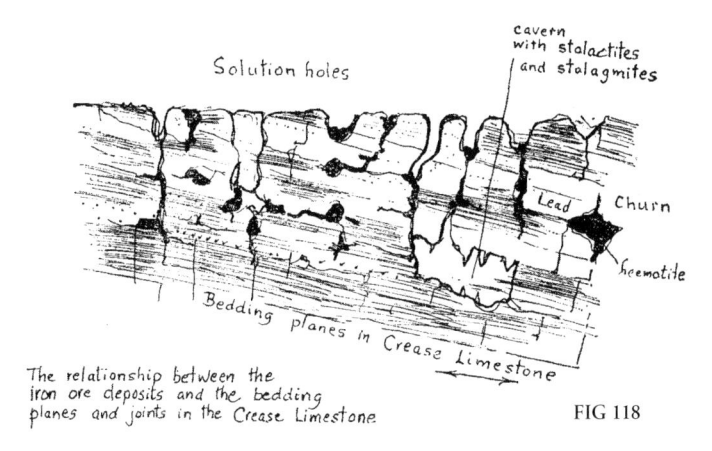

FIG 118 — The relationship between the iron ore deposits and the bedding planes and joints in the Crease Limestone.

the Crease Limestone for ore and found that it could be obtained from quite shallow workings in western Dean, whereas on the eastern side the ore went down into much deeper pockets. This is explained in Figures 116 and 117, from which it is obvious that the descending solutions could have penetrated much deeper into the highly-inclined strata on the eastern side of the Dean syncline. This also explains why there are such deep shafts on the east, eg, those at Shakemantle, Buckshaft and St Annals mines. Figure 118 shows how the iron-ore deposits are related to the joints and bedding planes in the Crease Limestone. It can be seen also that following a 'lead' of ore might bring one to a good churn, though sometimes it could lead to an underground cavern complete with stalactites and stalagmites. The ore seekers also knew that under the Coal Measure strata lean or barren ground was encountered – a point in favour of our theory. However, there is one area in the Coal Measures where iron ore was mined, and this is in Barnhill Plantation, near the Bixslade stone works at Cannop Ponds. The iron occurs as haematite along the joint-faces of the Pennant Sandstones and this mine was working as recently as the Second World War. On Barnhill Plantation and around Worcester Lodge a good deal of surface ore can be picked up but one must be careful not to confuse this with the scattered ore and cinders often found along old routeways. Perhaps various bands of clays and shales within the Coal Measures acted as barriers and prevented the iron solutions from descending into the limestones below.

The ore itself is haematite or ferric oxide, Fe_2O_3 and of high quality, for it is about 60 per cent pure iron. When hydrated, it becomes the common brown mineral called goethite. A good test in the field for haematite is that the finely ground powder is cherry red in colour. Geologists use a piece of unglazed porcelain known as a 'streak plate' which, when scratched with the ore, produces a red streak. If the streak is brown the mineral will be goethite. On breaking a crust of ore adhering to a limestone surface one often sees it gleaming with needle-like radiating crystals to which the apt name 'brush ore' was given by the miners. They found that if cinders from old iron workings were mixed with this brush ore a much tougher iron was produced. In places a more hydrated form of earthy ore known as 'ochre' was found and many tons of this discovered in Old Ham Mine were exported to paint manufacturers and for a time fetched a better price than the iron ore itself.

Mineral collectors may find it difficult to obtain good specimens of haematite and goethite in the various scowles described in the previous chapter, and one must remember that for many hundreds of years iron was the sole source of income for Dean miners. No ore meant no bread and butter and so, as we look around the scowles, it is not surprising that every crust of ore has been scraped off. Seeing pretty examples of haematite in the caverns, often with tiny stalactites of iron glistening all over with minute rhombs of calcite or dolomite, the writer prefers to leave them in place because of their educational value. Too many students of geology are inclined to use their hammers indiscriminately and would do well to appreciate that minerals are best seen in their natural surroundings rather than in a local museum.

Chapter 16
The Coal Measures: Scenery and Mining

IF reference is made to the map in Chapter 3, it will be seen that the strata of the Coal Measures occupy the central region of the Dean syncline. The basin is about ten miles long and six miles broad and most of it is Crown property under the control of the Forestry Commission.

The diagram, Figure 119, shows that the total thickness of strata is over 2,000 feet, yet a good deal of the thickest division, the Supra Pennant, is not exposed at the surface. This is because it fills up the central part of the basin around which it crops out rather concentrically. It will be seen that there are three main divisions consisting chiefly of sandstones, shales and grits with thin seams of coal. Many geological maps colour the outcrop of Coal Measures black as if to suggest that a good deal of the strata consist of coal seams. This gives a false impression for, in Dean, the sum total of all the coal seams is only some thirty feet. Therefore only about 1 per cent of the total thickness is actual coal and this is roughly true of all British coalfields. From the diagram, it can be seen that the Coleford High Delf seam, which has an average thickness of four feet, is the most important one, supplying some 97 per cent of the coal from the whole region.

Looking at the table of strata in Figure 119 we can expect to find the most spectacular scenery associated with the massive sandstones of the Pennant group, that is, high relief and deep valleys in contrast with the lower relief associated with the shales and thinly bedded sandstones in other series. On the eastern scarp of Dean, along the limestone ridge from Plump Hill south to near Ruspidge, one can look westward into the basin with its numerous sandstone ridges, and realise that the large town of Cinderford owes its development to coal mining. To the west of the town a long front of large coal tips separates it from the Forest, behind which are even bigger tips which characterise the landscape of central Dean. If we take the road from Cinderford direct to Speech House and continue to near the cross-roads at Cannop Ponds, looking westwards we can see the best example of Coal Measure scenery. Here the Forestry Commission has levelled out an old colliery tip to make a fine picnic ground, from which there are grand views to the west across the deep north-south valley eroded by Cannop Brook. This is the country of the Pennant Sandstone, with its typical steep slopes only partly covered by small plantations of

FIG 119

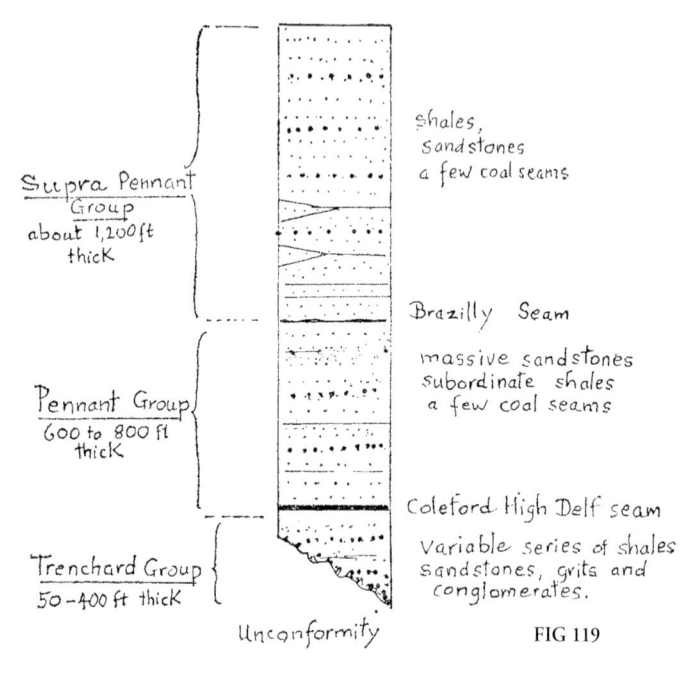

Supra Pennant Group — about 1,200 ft thick
- shales, sandstones, a few coal seams

Brazilly Seam

Pennant Group — 600 to 800 ft thick
- massive sandstones, subordinate shales, a few coal seams

Coleford High Delf seam

Trenchard Group — 50–400 ft thick
- Variable series of shales, sandstones, grits and conglomerates.

Unconformity

---

large oaks, the rest being at present planted with young trees so that it is possible to enjoy distant vistas into other branching valleys beyond.

The name 'slade' is given to such deep valleys and Wimberry Slade, shown in Figure 120, is perhaps the best of them. For relative solitude and forest splendour, this valley and the one occupied by the Greathough Brook near Brierley are recommended. The change of vegetation is remarkable for the acid soils formed on the sandstones favour the growth of such typical grass plants as the Common Bent (*Agrostis tenuis*), Yorkshire Fog (*Holcus lanatus*) and Red Fescue (*Festuca rubra*), whilst in between the stands of oak trees is the ubiquitous bracken. Wimberry Slade is made more interesting by an occasional solitary hut of a miner who has taken advantage of the stratification to drive a gallery or level into the hillside to get at a coal seam. In places at the entrance to the adit the seam of coal can be seen, while in the waste rock nearby excellent fossil roots of

The Coal Measures: Scenery and Mining

Carboniferous trees (*Stigmaria*) can be picked up.

At the head of the valley there is an old quarry in the Pennant Sandstone, so called after the Welsh word 'pennant' meaning valley head, for it is in such places in South Wales that the sandstones were quarried. Good specimens of fossil plants can be obtained from the large tip-heap of the derelict Cannop colliery which once employed 800 men. Spontaneous combustion takes place in some of the tips and in winter, steam sometimes issues from the slopes. After some years the internal heat, a form of slow oxidation, changes the blue-grey shales to a red colour in the interior and today there is even a demand for the 'red rocks' from old tip heaps. Some of the oldest waste tips, looking like miniature mountains clothed with trees and grass, are good picnic spots and provide fine viewpoints from which one can see other large tips looming up like ancient volcanoes.

Throughout Dean it is easy to pick out the Coal Measure strata at the junction with the rocks of the Lower Carboniferous series or where they rest on the Devonian. Figure 121 illustrates this in the Ruardean locality. The village itself is built on the thin shales and sandstones of the Trenchard group, but the land begins to rise quite steeply to the south as soon as the massive sandstones of the Pennant group crop out. At the base of these

FIG 120 Wimberry Slade A deep valley in the Pennant sandstone. galleries or adits are driven into the hillside to reach seams of coal

is the Coleford High Delf seam of coal and here and there remains of small coal mines may still be seen. The village school is close by an old coal pit in this seam. At Edge End, near Coleford, similar scenery to that shown in Figure 121 can be seen, where once again the Coal Measures rest on Lower Dolomite and other strata in the series. There are numerous quarries in the Pennant Sandstone all along the hillside around Ruardean Hill which, at 951 feet, is the highest point in Dean. If one follows the B4228 road Ruardean to Kerne Bridge the scenery just outside Ruardean contrasts with that on the Coal Measures and Lower Dolomite. Figure 121 also shows how water released at the junction of the clays of the Trenchard group with the Lower Dolomite has eroded a deep valley leading down to the Wye.

To study the Pennant Sandstone in detail and to appreciate its importance in the building industry it is essential to visit the three large quarries at Bixhead in Barnhill Plantation, west of Cannop Ponds. The best way is to follow the B4226 road to near Worcester Lodge. Figure 122 shows the great quarry cliff face exposing some 120 feet of massive sandstones, where three large electric cranes haul the stone to the surface. The rock in the first ten feet from the top is very shattered and to avoid a type of stone that will flake in frosty weather it is necessary to

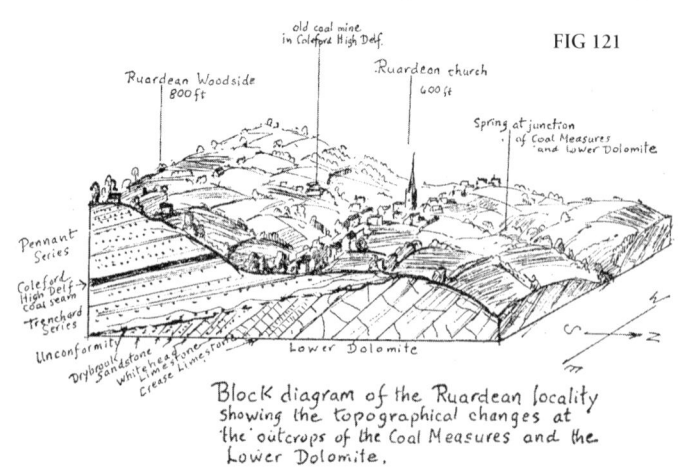

FIG 121

Block diagram of the Ruardean locality showing the topographical changes at the outcrops of the Coal Measures and the Lower Dolomite.

The Coal Measures: Scenery and Mining

FIG 122

One of the quarries at Bixhead Pennant Sandstone. Notice the current bedding to the left

quarry deep down. Until recently, the stone was mined and today the visitor can enter these places, which are like large underground halls, from the quarry floor. This was a dangerous method of working the stone and one can see how huge slabs of sandstone forming the roof of the 'hall' were bolted together to prevent rockfalls occurring.

The sandstones are often irregularly bedded and among them are fine examples of current bedding indicating deposition in ancient river deltas some 280 million years ago. Interbedded with the sandstones one can see conglomerates containing occasional pebbles of coal here and there. Some of the strata consist of thin beds of shale and a coal seam about two inches thick is visible in one section of the quarry face. In the more massive sandstones can be found the casts of quite large tree trunks of the type *Sigillaria*. The whole cliff face here and in the neighbouring quarries of Bixhead demonstrates the most important factor in the formation of coal, viz.

rapid burial of vegetation, and in this case by masses of sand; the massive sandstones of the Pennant group indicating rapid and continuous sedimentation.

The fine quality of the sandstone in the Bixhead quarries adds to its commercial value, and for this reason and because of the variations in colour, it is much in demand by builders. A good deal of the sandstone is yellow-brown owing to the presence of the mineral limonite, a hydrated ferric oxide which forms a coating on the sand grains in the rock. The grey colouring of some of the sandstones is due to the presence among the sand grains of very finely divided particles of carbonaceous material derived from eroded coal seams. The grey colour is also due to the ferrous compounds of iron that tend to form in the reducing environment produced by plant debris. When a sediment contains much organic matter, such as plant remains, the ferric compounds are robbed of their oxygen and, since ferrous compounds tend to be grey, the reddish-brown rocks assume a grey colour. Some of the sandstones are blue-grey and this may be due to variations of the above two factors or to the presence of finely divided iron sulphide.

The variety of colours in the sandstones make them highly prized for their value as ornamental stone. The stone is sent down to the Bixslade stone works, situated about a mile distant on the road to Parkend at the southern end of Cannop Ponds. This is still a busy place where the great slabs of sandstone are sawn up into blocks for buildings, monuments, fireplaces, etc. Some of the buildings constructed recently in this colourful stone include the University College of Wales, Aberystwyth, the nuclear power station at Berkeley, University College, London, the Shire Hall, Gloucester and many large bank buildings.

The right to work coal or iron in the Forest of Dean is vested in the local inhabitants, who can qualify as free miners provided an applicant has worked for 'a year and a day' in a Forest coal or iron mine. The right to mine an area is known as a gale and the deputy gaveller, whose office is at Coleford, is the official to whom applications must be made. An investigation in 1967 showed that most of the nineteen mines then producing coal were employing only three to five men. If these coal mines were plotted on the geological map shown in Chapter 3 it would show them to be all marginal to the main basin, with none working in the central portion, ie, the outcrop of the Supra Pennant. This is because all the old mines in Central Dean are waterlogged and the reason for this was explained in the geological sections in Chapter 3. The Dean

The Coal Measures: Scenery and Mining

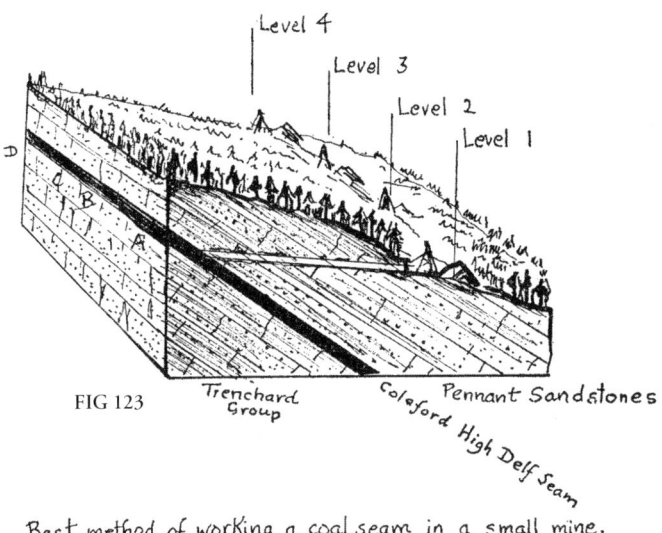

FIG 123 — Trenchard Group, Coleford High Delf Seam, Pennant Sandstones. Levels 1, 2, 3, 4.

Best method of working a coal seam in a small mine.
1. Drive in a level above the coal. Level 1
2. Water will drain out of mine
3. Work out coal at A.
4. Drive in levels at 2, 3, and 4 to work B, C, and D.
5. Next excavate vertical shafts lower down hillside.

This is the situation near Cinderford, where there are steeply inclined strata associated with the Staple Edge Monocline.

basin is an asymmetrical syncline which allows water to collect in the central basin; in fact, it is known that any shaft penetrating to within eighty-five feet above sea level will encounter underground water. For example, at Ruardean Hill, the highest point at 951 feet, a small two-man mine is operating and if the shaft goes down 866 feet waterlogged conditions will be reached. It is this water problem that presents the main obstacle to mining: in the old days of steam engine pumps it was one of the factors that led to the closing of most of the large collieries. Today, electric pumps are much more efficient but they are expensive for the small two-man type of mine. The diagram, Figure 123, shows how one miner gets at the coal face by a method which miners used as far back as 1870 when the idea

FIG 124

An exposed coal seam in the Supra Pennant Series. Wet Wood near Cannop Ponds (Beechenhurst Wood)

was 'to get above the coal' and so prevent surface water from getting into the mine.

Along the eastern side of Dean, owing to the Staple Edge monocline, the Coal Measures dip very steeply and the gales are mostly located on the western side where the dips are not so steep and where levels can be driven into the hillside; this is known as adit mining. As in the old days, the Coleford High Delf seams remains the most sought after; and this is another reason why most of the mines working today are marginal to the central basin. Some miners only work at week-ends in their small mines and hold other jobs during the week. They have no problem at all in selling the coal for, once they have put it out on the surface, the National Coal Board

The Coal Measures: Scenery and Mining

is responsible for its collection and sale. Some goes to power stations, eg, Lydney and Gloucester, and only about one-tenth is used for house coal. Walking along a forest road one may suddenly come upon a small tip of blue-grey shale, a pile of timber and an old car engine hauling up tubs of coal. The man down-under prefers to work by the light of a carbide lamp as it spreads the light better than an electric lamp, and this is permissible as Dean coalfield is classified as a naked light area. There are only two records of pit explosions, one at Brierley in 1927 and the other at Ruspidge in 1950.

Visitors to the area would be well advised not to ask to go down a mine. It upsets the workings of the pit and in any case there is little to be seen with a small lamp. It is far better to find a place where a coal seam can be seen in the open, although this is not easy as the soft strata soon crumble away when exposed and become overgrown with grass. At the present time, 1968, there are only three such places. North of Cannop Ponds and close to the old Cannop Colliery, is the Beechenhurst Wood pit. The coal seam in the Supra Pennant known as the 'Twenty Inch' is visible in a forest clearing and the sketch, Figure 124, shows this seam. As in all seams of coal, there is an underlying seat-earth of clay which is the fossil soil on which the Carboniferous trees grew, so that in it we find the *Stigmaria* roots. To the miners, this fireclay is known as 'clod', whilst the name 'duns' is given to the mudstone overlying the coal seam. If a coal seam becomes divided into two by a band of clod, the division is known as a 'leat' and some are shown in the diagram, Figure 119. A coal seam known as the Yorkley can be seen at the entrance to an adit mine in the upper part of Wimberry Slade, and the tip heap close by is perhaps the best in the Forest for *Stigmaria* specimens. Another seam of coal is exposed in a cutting in the forest road through Ten-Acre Wood close to Primrose Hill, north of Lydney. This is the Trenchard seam shown in Figure 125. Finally, in the cricket field at Whitecroft, north of Lydney, there is an exposure of the Parkend High Delf seam belonging to the Supra Pennant group.

There are, of course, many places in Dean where a coal seam can be exposed after a few minutes work with a shovel, but for advice about this local miners should be consulted for their great wealth of knowledge on the various coal seams. Many of them worked as young lads in the old days when the large collieries such as those at Cannop, Northern United, Eastern United and Princess Royal were operating, each employing up to 800 men. The last big colliery closed down in 1966. Now, many of these former workers in the mines exercise their rights as free miners to operate small pits and can tell the visitor the exact location of the fourteen seams in the Forest.

Quite recently a Gloucester firm, using a gale, has started an open-cast mining venture at Steam Mills, north of Cinderford. This is an area on Nofold Green where the land is scarred by many old surface workings. Operations began in 1967 and three seams are being worked in the Supra Pennant group. These seams are apparently separated by about ten feet of blue clay, and during spells of rainy weather the large tractors and excavating machines flounder in the sticky mud. The whole operation is highly mechanised, the coal being excavated by machines and fed into a conveyor belt which tips it into waiting lorries. This work may go on for another year, after which all the ground will be levelled over and seeded with grass. The Forestry Commission have allowed this rather unsightly and disfiguring operation because formerly the area was waste ground and it is hoped that when, in due course, the land is restored it will look better than it did originally.

Mention must also be made of the brickworks a few hundred yards north of the open-cast mining. Here the factory uses the same blue clays in the Supra Pennant that are causing trouble in the open-cast mines. This blue clay is used for making very high-quality bricks for use in public buildings. By the admixture of various sands, grey, red and purple bricks are produced and the factory itself is unique in being about the only one in Britain that still makes bricks by hand. Another brickworks nearby utilises the shale from a large old mine tip-heap.

Finally, we must explain why the National Coal Board has closed down all its collieries in Dean. There are a number of reasons. The seams were in many cases nearing exhaustion and it became uneconomical to continue working them in the way that had been usual in a large colliery. Also, water in the mines became a big problem, in addition to which there were labour difficulties. As pits began to close, the young men went into other industries, leaving the older ones in the remaining collieries. Some pits had troubles with 'washouts', areas where partly-formed coal had been washed away by river channels in Carboniferous times. Nevertheless, it is still possible to make a small mine pay its way, provided the water problem can be solved, though many miners today, once underground, find that much of the coal has already been taken out

FIG 125 — The Trenchard Coal Seam exposed on a Forest road in Ten Acre Wood north of Lydney, near Primrose Hill

by previous mining. Free mining can also involve a considerable expenditure. If, for example, a solitary miner can dig out say, twenty tons of coal during a week-end at £4 a ton, his £80 of income has to be set against the high cost of timber and machinery. For all of them today it is very much a matter of make do and mend.

Chapter 17

The Origin of the Coal in the Forest of Dean

ABOUT 280 million years ago in the upper part of the Carboniferous period, a land mass extending from Wales to Belgium separated a series of coastal swamps that lay both to the north and south of this land. A sketch map showing the conjectured palaeogeography of the time is seen in Figure 126. There were perhaps embayments in the Dean and Bristol regions and around the coastal regions were vast swamps covered with dense forest vegetation in a hot and humid climate something like that of the Ganges delta today. The trees were mainly giant club mosses called Lycopods, eg, *Sigillaria* and *Lepidodendron*, reaching to a height of 100 to 150 feet. There were also horse tail trees, eg, *Calamites* and fern-like plants called *Pteridosperms*, eg, *Alethopteris, Neuropteris* and *Annularia*. These latter grew on higher mud banks, for we find these fossil plants in the shales overlying the coal seams.

As the trees fell into the stagnating swamp, anaerobic bacteria secured the oxygen they needed by taking it from the oxygen-rich compounds of which plant tissue or cellulose ($C_6H_{10}O_5$) was the chief material. In doing this the bacteria released free hydrogen which combined with the sulphate residues of organic matter to produce the gas, sulphuretted hydrogen, H_2S. This toxic gas dissolved in the water and soon destroyed all life in the swamp. Also the gas combined with the ever

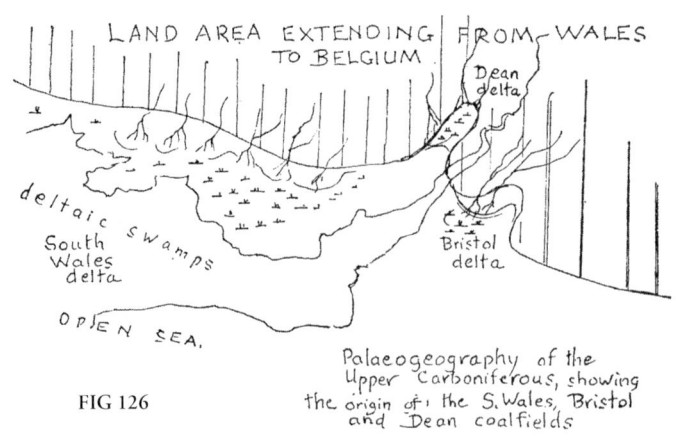

FIG 126

Palaeogeography of the Upper Carboniferous, showing the origin of the S. Wales, Bristol and Dean coalfields

The Origins of Coal in the Forest of Dean

FIG 127

roots = Stigmaria — Lepidodendron giant Lycopod 150 ft; Sigillaria; Calamites, giant horsetail tree; Amphibia; giant dragonflies 30 inches wing span; Pteridosperms e.g. Neuropteris living on mud flats

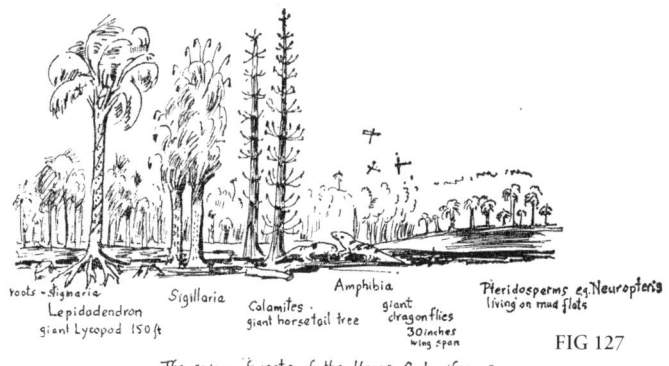

The swamp forests of the Upper Carboniferous
A scene in the Dean Delta about 290 million years ago

present soluble iron compounds to form iron sulphide, which is sometimes finely disseminated, producing a black or blue-grey shale, but often occurs as the brassy-looking mineral, pyrite, frequently found in shale. It is also common in coal and its yellow brightness gives rise to the name 'fool's gold'.

But to return to our swamps where the vegetation is now partly reduced to a carbonaceous mass of jelly-like, putrefying matter. The bacterial attack has now ceased, brought to an end by the toxic conditions of its own environment. It must be remembered that although bacteria leave behind no fossil trace, their work in the formation of coal, of ore bodies, and other formations in sedimentary rocks cannot be over-emphasised. Figure 127 shows the type of vegetation which flourished around the coastal swamps, and the soils on which these forests grew became compacted to form the seat earth found under the coal seams.

The land mass to the north, however, was very unstable, and as the forests were nearly at sea level even a slight depression would allow the sea to flow in and change the environment from a delta swamp to a lagoon. At the same time the Wales-Belgium land mass began to rise and this see-saw kind of movement resulted in rivers bringing down vast quantities of sand, so that the accumulated plant debris of the swamp soon became buried under thick layers of sand. This process can be deduced from the Pennant sandstones of the Bixhead quarries. The buried forests soon changed into peat but the actual process of the change from peat to coal (coalification) is not yet fully

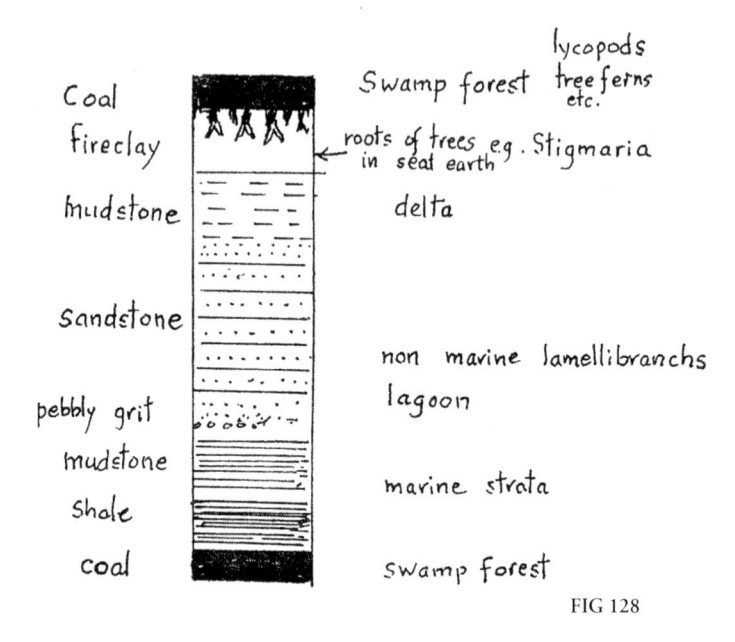

```
                              lycopods
                Swamp forest  tree ferns
 Coal                          etc.
 fireclay       ←roots of trees e.g. Stigmaria
                  in seat earth
 mudstone        delta


 sandstone
                 non marine lamellibranchs
 pebbly grit     lagoon
 mudstone
 shale           marine strata
 coal            swamp forest
```

FIG 128

Diagram showing the types of strata miners usually find between coal seams. This unit, called a CYCLOTHEM is repeated many times in the Coal Measures.

understood. It probably took many millions of years to change from peat through lignite to bituminous coal. Very often the land and sea movements were reversed so that more swamp forests grew on the sand flats which, in turn, became buried again.

In this way a kind of cycle of sedimentation was repeated. Figure 128 shows something that is familiar to many coal miners. In Dean, they find that beneath the coal is the clod, a fossil soil of clayey texture, which contains many tree stumps in an upright position indicating such rapid burial that there was not enough time for them to be destroyed in situ. Above the coal is found the 'duns', a shaly kind of mudstone in which are found freshwater mussels, eg, *Anthraconauta* and remains of fern-like plants. This indicates the burial of the forest debris. Above this are found sandstones, sediments which were brought down by rivers and buried in the swamp. One finds this repeated so often in the Coal Measures that the term 'cyclothem' is used for such a cycle of sedimentation. In the Forest of Dean, however, evidence of marine sediments in the Coal Measures is lacking and perhaps this area may have been under estuarine conditions (Figure 129). When rivers made their way through the delta swamps, channels would be cut right through the buried vegetation and this is the explanation of the so called 'wash out' that the miners complain about when they operate a gale and find the coal seam just disappears, ie, washed out by ancient rivers.

Was the Forest of Dean region at this time, say 280 million years ago, close to the earth's equator, or had tropical climate spread all over the earth? In the former case some geologists believe in the theory of Continental Drift which presupposes that the continents were once closer together and lay near the equator, but since then have drifted apart. An explanation, perhaps, of the tropical vegetation in England during the Carboniferous period.

Finally, one must take note of Chapter 3 in which is mentioned the great Hercynian orogeny, for at the end of the swamp forests period arid conditions set in. Great earth movements folded all the Carboniferous strata, and subsequent erosion separated the Coal Measures into basins, so that today in Britain our coalfields are separated by these folds and, of course, after such folding many thousands of feet of Coal Measure strata were eroded away. It is fortunate that Britain had these swamp forests millions of years

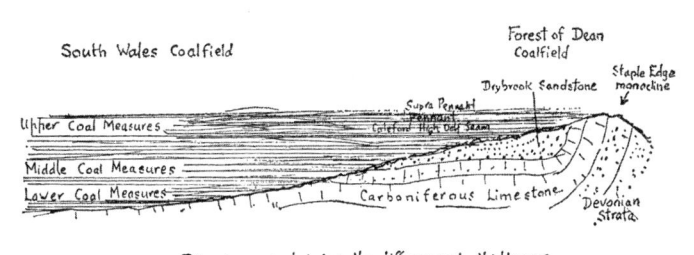

FIG 129

Diagram explaining the differences in thicknesses and position of the Coal Measures between the Forest of Dean and South Wales

FIG 130

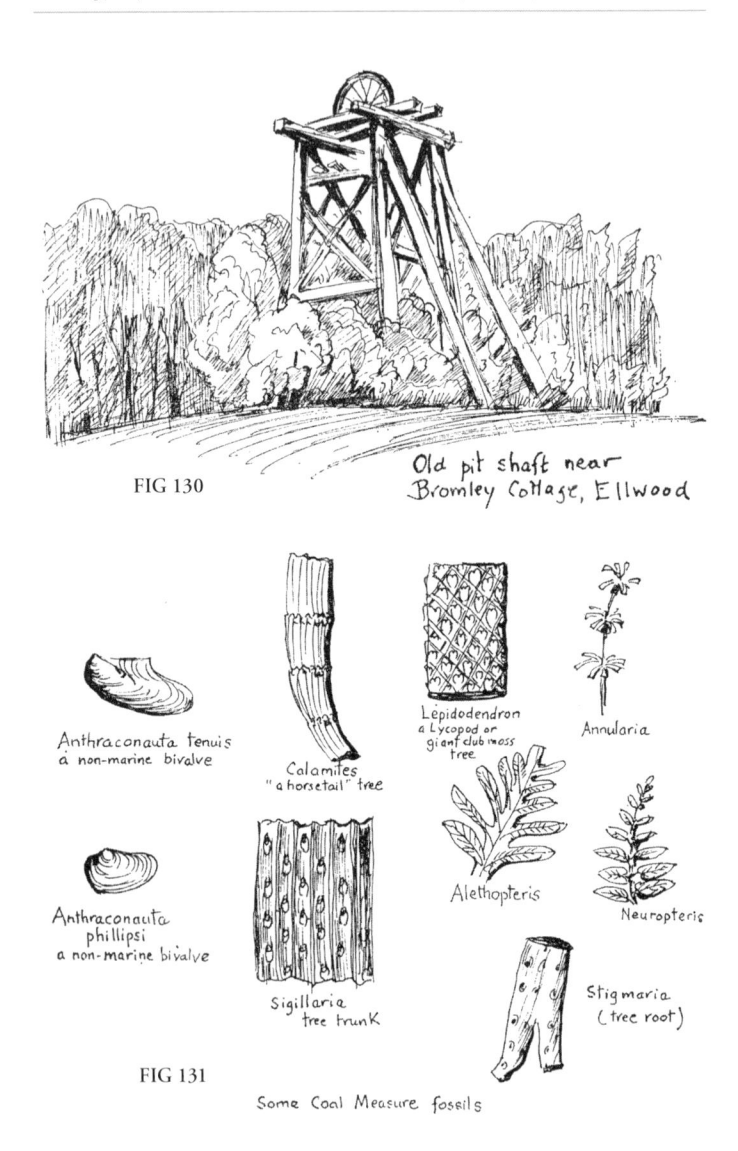

Old pit shaft near Bromley Cottage, Ellwood

Anthraconauta tenuis
a non-marine bivalve

Anthraconauta phillipsi
a non-marine bivalve

Calamites
"a horsetail" tree

Lepidodendron
a Lycopod or giant club moss tree

Annularia

Alethopteris

Neuropteris

Sigillaria
tree trunk

Stigmaria
(tree root)

FIG 131

Some Coal Measure fossils

ago, for it was coal that provided the energy for steam power during industrial revolution.

The Forest of Dean escaped the spoliation of the countryside which took place in the other industrial areas on the coalfields of Britain and today it remains the prettiest coalfield of all. Let us hope that the rumours of starting yet more open-cast mining operations in Dean are false, for this would gravely affect the amenities of the Forest. The sketch Figure 130 of an old coal mine being gradually smothered in trees may be regarded as a true symbol of the decline of the coal industry.

The finest ramble for the industrial archaeologist who appreciates good scenery with his study starts from Ruardean Hill and follows the deep valley leading southwards to near Brierley by Astonbridge Hill. This leads by Forest roads into the Greathough Brook valley and on through an ever deepening valley to Lydbrook. On the way there are many old shafts, quarries, remnant tracks of old railway lines and adjacent tip-heaps. At many places along the route fossil plant remains are to be found and collectors of these should take note of the types shown in Figure 131.

Chapter 18
Some Geological Curiosities

OMITTED from previous chapters as not being directly relevant to the subject under discussion, the following items may add to the interest of visits made to the places concerned.

STRUCTURAL GEOLOGY IN TIDENHAM QUARRY

In this quarry in the Lower Dolomite, which dips at 65 degrees to the west, we are looking at the eastern limb of the Tidenham syncline, and when strata are pushed up at steep angles like this there is a tendency for them to slide down under the influence of gravity. This will only occur when the top of the anticline is eroded off, weakening the whole structure, but remember that it is a question of time, for the fold occurred some 270 million years ago, since when much of the top part of the structure has been eroded off. In some parts of the quarry one can see large exposures of bedding planes with minor folds and this seems to have occurred in weaker strata as shown in Figure 132.

SMALL FOLDS IN LIMESTONE

It is often difficult for the beginner to realize that an apparently brittle rock like limestone can bend and fold, but here again it is a question of time and thickness of overburden. Figures 133 and 134 illustrate a small anticline in the Lower Limestone Shale. This series often shows limestones interbedded with shales and these latter, being weaker, tend to crumple into small folds against the more resistant limestone bands. The section shown in Figure 133 is rarely seen but in the vicinity many dome structures can be recognized along forest roads in the Bishops Wood area near Kerne Bridge.

A FAULTED ANTICLINE

Chapter 3 dealt with structures in Dean and it was stated that faults do not very much affect the relief. A fault is a fracture in the rocks along which movement has taken place and faults tend to occur in any strata, whether folded, tilted or horizontal. A good example of the effect on topography of a fault associated with a fold is to be seen at Bircham Wood about half a mile east of Newland Church. This hill towers to a height over 700 feet and dominates the village; viewed from near Clearwell it is a very bold topographical feature. The geological sketch map, Figure 135, shows that it is a fold plunging to the north, the southern half of which has snapped off along a fault and

Some Geological Curiosities

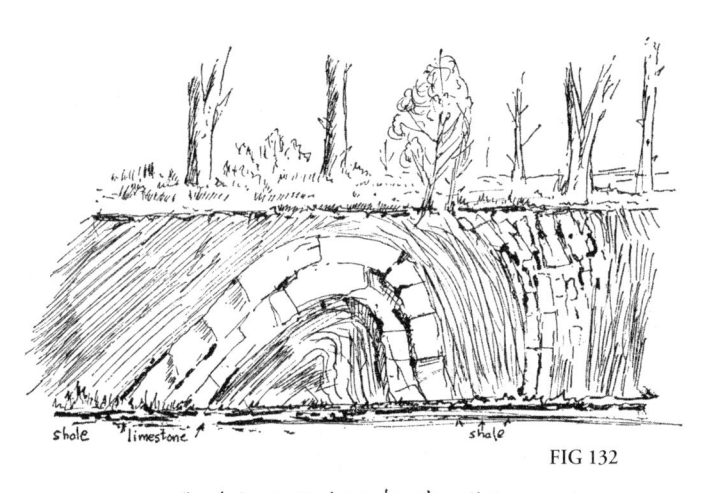

FIG 132

small anticline in the Lower Limestone Shale in Grove Wood, between Kerne Bridge and Lydbrook

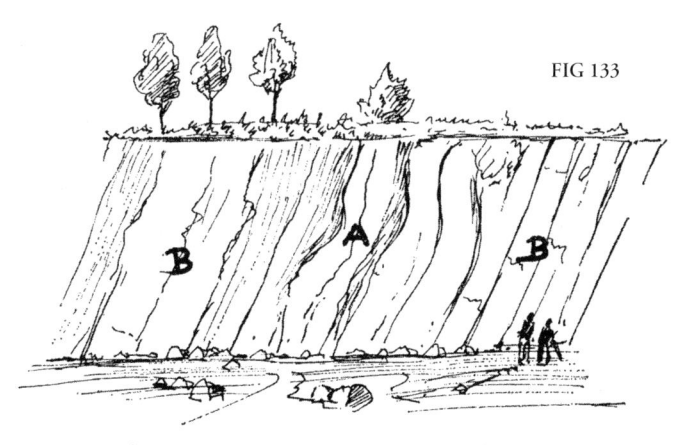

FIG 133

Tidenham Quarry. Lower Dolomite – dip 65°
Minor fold at A caused by gravity sliding, between two massive beds of dolomite rock at B

FIG 134

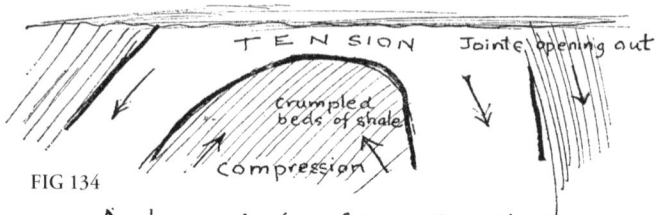

Analysis of sharp fold in Grove Wood. This anticline is asymmetrical. The right limb of the fold is nearly vertical

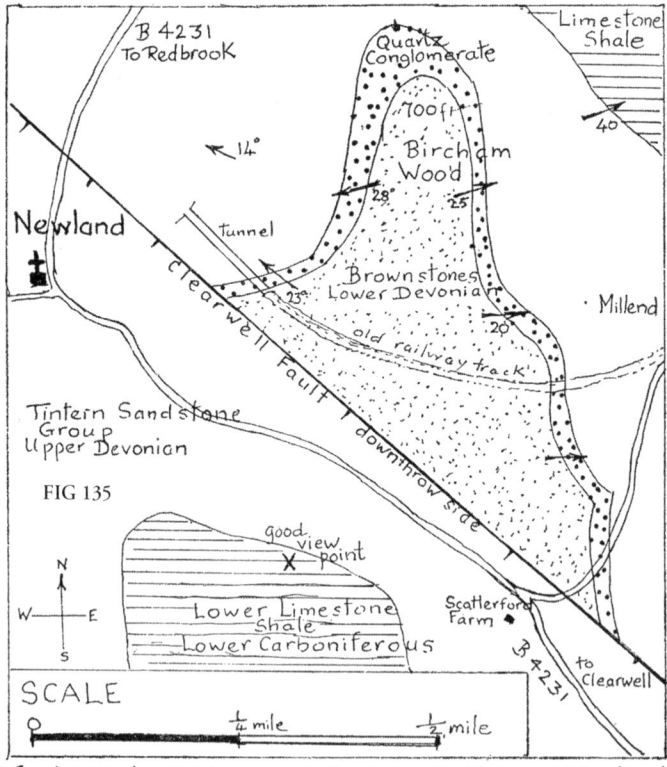

FIG 135

Geological sketch map of faulted anticline near Newland

been displaced downwards so that the younger strata are preserved to the south of the fault. The angles of dip are shown and indicate that it is rather a symmetrical anticline, about half a mile across at the fault zone. The block diagram Figure 136 shows the nature of the fault and that part of the valley leading from Clearwell to Newland is a fault valley, but the diagram does not show the real reason for the high bold relief feature of Bircham Wood. Hence, the second block diagram Figure 137 reveals the structure of the hill by vertical cuts taken parallel to the fault. It can be seen also that the crest of the hill is the core of the anticline, formed of massive Brownstones while Quartz Conglomerate plays only a minor role in the topography. After examining the 'baby' anticlines, this much bigger one can now be investigated by walking along the old railway track to the tunnel shown on the map, Figure 135. From the hill, one can obtain grand views of the abandoned meander channel of the Wye in the Newland area.

JOINT SYSTEMS

Looking at rock surfaces in quarries, one can detect a certain pattern in the system of joints developed on bedding planes. In any given locality the joints tend to take two main directions, and Shakemantle Quarry is one of the best exposures to show such joint systems. In the first place they are due to stresses and strains set up in the rock as it dries out. The lithification process took place not long after deposition and so regular joints formed as the rock began to shrink owing to loss of volume. Later, these Joints would be accentuated on folding, but other factors might introduce a new set of joints. Figure 138 shows some the vast bedding surfaces exposed in Shakemantle Quarry near Ruspidge.

RAFTS

These are lumps of sandstone containing sections of tree trunks. Originally, the fallen logs floated about in a sandy lagoon in the coal swamps of the Upper Carboniferous period. Soon, the logs became covered with sand just as they piled up in criss-cross fashion in the ancient lagoon. The cores of the decayed trunks were filled with sand while the outer parts were converted to coal. The best specimens of these fossilised logs are in the large pit heap of the old Northern United Colliery near Nailbridge (see Figures 139 and 140).

SLICKENSIDES

An old quarry opposite Bearse Farm, about half a mile-north east of St Briavels, shows one cliff

FIG 136

Block diagram of a fault block near Newland.

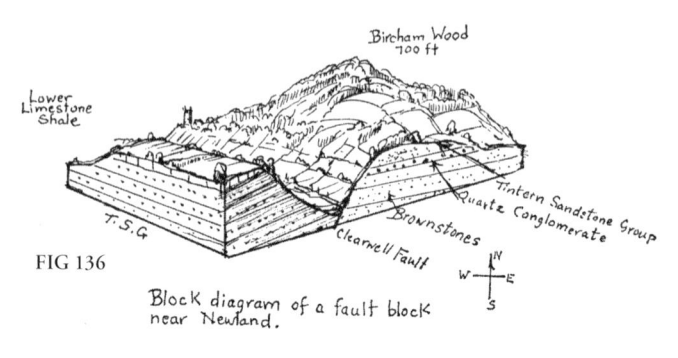

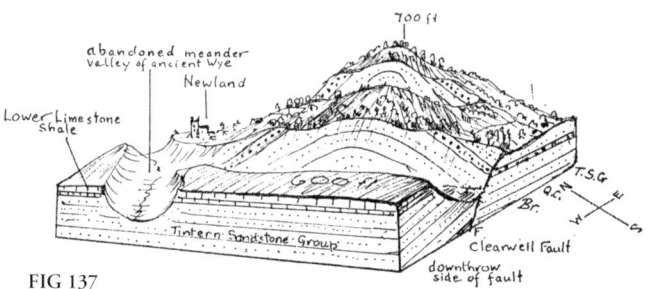

Labels: Bircham Wood 700 ft, Lower Limestone Shale, T.S.G., Clearwell Fault, Brownstones, Quartz Conglomerate, Tintern Sandstone Group

FIG 137

Block diagram of the faulted anticline near Newland.

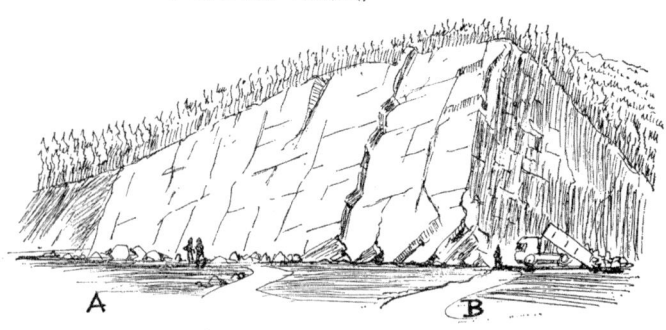

Labels: 700 ft, abandoned meander valley of ancient Wye, Newland, Lower Limestone Shale, Tintern Sandstone Group, T.S.G., Br., Q.C., Clearwell Fault, downthrow side of fault

FIG 138

Shakemantle Quarry – Ruspidge
The joint system in bedding planes of the Lower Dolomite
Bedding planes A—B

face with many parallel horizontal grooves called 'slickensides', and in places the travertine (redeposited limestone) which was deposited along the joint planes has nearly all been scraped off. This is evidence of rock movements when one mass of limestone has moved against another adjoining mass, as shown in Figure 141. The travertine could have been formed in geologically recent times and the rock movements also could have taken place recently. Rock masses tend to move along master joints in the limestone and this introduces a new set of joints, known as shear joints. Although the major Armorican earth movements occurred some 270 million years ago, renewed movements have frequently occurred since then.

CLINTS AND GRIKES

In many of the villages in the Chepstow area, people like to put ornamental stones on top of stone walls surrounding their cottages and bungalows. The most popular seem to be weird pieces of a white limestone. These are found under the soil lying on top of the Drybrook Limestone in the Wintour's Leap and Woodcroft areas. Acid waters from the soil percolate downwards into the joints and widen them by solution, and these are called 'grikes' in the Pennines. The flat areas between the grikes, called 'clints', have mall solution hollows, so that when solution is far advanced in both clints and grikes bizarre-shaped pieces of rock are produced. Later, these become detached and are found in rock debris in the subsoil. Figure 142 shows the use and origin of the stone.

DENDRITIC HAEMATITE

A good deal of the Lower Dolomite is impregnated with haematite, hence the pinkish colour of the rock, but in places much stronger iron solutions have seeped along tiny cracks and rock surfaces and the partial crystallisation has caused tree-like patterns resembling a miniature landscape with trees. The process of formation is similar to that in which frost patterns form on window panes. The old quarry near Stowe is the best collecting place for dendritic haematite. Figure 143 shows a good specimen about ten inches in length.

DISAPPEARING RIVERS AND POTHOLES

There is a good deal of surface water on the Coal Measures but, when streams flow off these strata on to areas of limestone, there is a tendency for them to disappear down gaping joints that have been widened out by solution. Then the rivers will continue underground until they finally emerge in springs, usually in the shale bands of the Lower Limestone Shale. The one

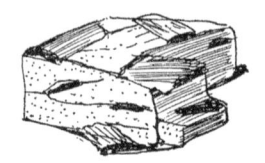

RAFTS Sections of tree trunks embedded in sandstone Coal Measures
FIG 139

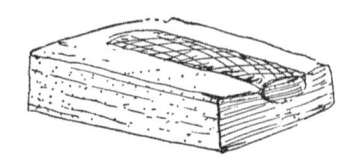

Cast of Lepidodendron trunk in Pennant Sandstone
FIG 140

FIG 141

Slickensides.
Quarry in Lower Limestone Shale opposite Bearse Farm, St. Briavels

Solution of limestone under the soil
e.g. Woodcroft Quarry north of Chepstow

Queer shaped limestone rocks as stone wall ornaments. Chepstow area

FIG 142

Clints and grikes in limestone

at Joyford Mill shown in Figure 144 has been investigated by the Forest of Dean Caving Society and, by using dyestuffs, members have found that the water in this sinkhole reaches the Wye near Symond's Yat. This is interesting because one can follow the same dry valley illustrated in Figure 144 northwards to Brooks Head Grove to a powerful spring from which a stream flows over the Lower Limestone Shale and finally reaches the Wye opposite English Bicknor. This stream is in no way connected with the one which disappeared into the sinkhole by Joyford Mill. Hoarthorns Farm, half a mile east of Joyford Mill, and Dunderhole Farm near Bishops Wood are two other examples of sinkholes but the one at Joyford Mill is by far the best in the whole region.

Swallets or swallow holes are just deep holes formed by solution of the limestone and today most of those in Dean show no sign of underground water. During the Pleistocene period there were wetter periods, probably lasting for many thousands of years, but owing to diminishing rainfall in the last 15,000 years, the level of underground water is now far lower than the deepest of these swallet holes. These holes tend to be in a series along the floor of a now dry valley, suggesting the course of an ancient river that flowed at times from one hole to another. Swallow holes may be found in Willscroft Wood between Bearse Farm and St Briavels, and in the upper part of Slade Brook about a quarter of a mile northwest of Bearse Farm. In the latter, the underground water flows on the shales of the Lower Limestone but emerges in numerous springs close to the junction with the Tintern Sandstone group of the Upper Devonian. Following the Slade brook down a steep-sided valley to Mork and on to Bigsweir, one can make a fascinating study of a rejuvenated river valley. Two other places for swallow holes are at 'Piccadilly', about a quarter of a mile west of Wynd Cliff, and near Parsons Allotment, east of Tidenham Chase.

CRINOIDS

Many beginners in geology like to visit places where there is an abundance of fossils. These are easily found in exposures of the Lower Limestone shale, for one of the ways to detect its outcrop is by the presence of crinoidal limestone. A piece of the rock is shown in one of the sketches in Figure 145. The tiny discs are scattered throughout the rock and all are pierced with a tiny hole. The segments represent the collapsed column of the stem of a sea animal known popularly as a 'stone lily'. These animals led mostly a fixed life in those times and lived together in large colonies

FIG 143

Dendritic haematite on a piece of limestone from an old quarry near Stow

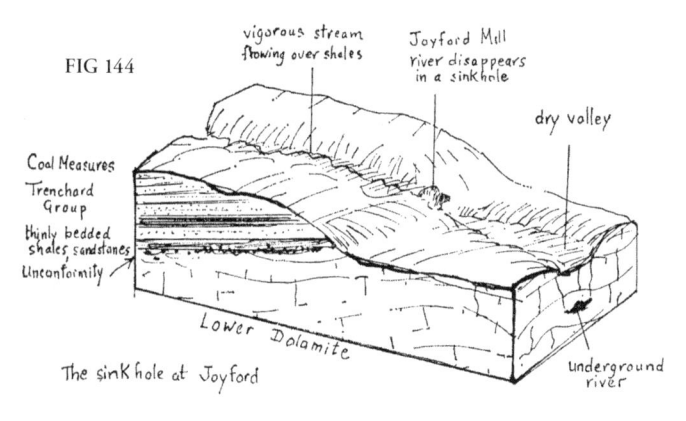

FIG 144

The sinkhole at Joyford

Labels: vigorous stream flowing over shales; Joyford Mill river disappears in a sinkhole; dry valley; Coal Measures; Trenchard Group; thinly bedded shales sandstones; Unconformity; Lower Dolomite; underground river

on the sea floor. It is because of this sessile and gregarious mode of life that we find so many of the fossil stem parts (columnals) together in the rock. When polished, a crinoidal limestone makes a very pretty ornamental stone. The best localities for crinoids are the old quarry opposite Bearse Farm near St Briavels and some old quarries south of Reeds Paper Mill, near Lower Lydbrook.

THE ICHTHYOSAURUS

One often hears from local gossip in the area along the Severn between Lydney and Blakeney that, somewhere on the banks of the river, there is a fossil marine reptile known as Ichthyosaurus.

FIG 145

pinnules, arm, colyx, columnal, segments of the column

a piece of crinoidal limestone from the Lower Limestone Shale

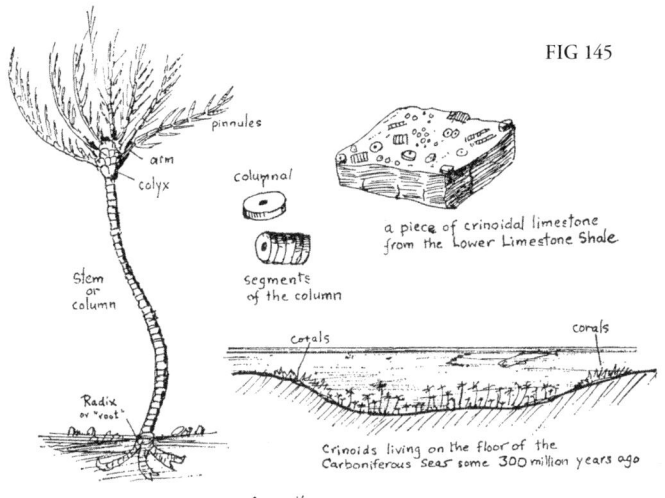

stem or column

Radix or "root"

A crinoid in position of growth on the sea floor.

corals — corals

Crinoids living on the floor of the Carboniferous seas some 300 million years ago

CRINOIDS

More recently, it has been reported as now lying deep in the mud of the foreshore. This marine reptile lived in the Jurassic period some 170 million years ago and parts of the skeleton are found in exposures of the Lower Lias Clay, especially on both sides of the Severn at Awre and Hock Cliff, Fretheme. The sketch, Figure 146, is a reconstruction to remind visitors what to look for.

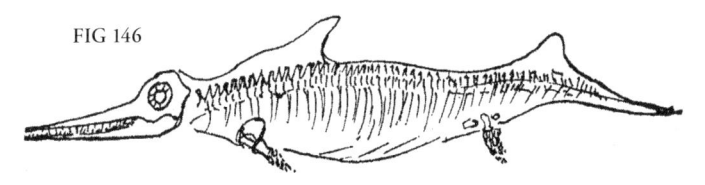

FIG 146

Ichthyosaurus — a marine reptile, reconstruction found in the Lower Jurassic Lower Lias Clay in Gloucestershire

SUN CRACKS

During the Devonian period, there were many inland lakes whose shores consisted of extensive mud flats. The drying of the mud caused shrinkage and so tension joints due to the decrease in volume were formed. These joints tend to become vertical fractures making an angle of 120 degrees with each other, so that if the centres of contraction are equally spaced, the cracks or joints will radiate out from these equidistant centres. In this way, when desiccation is complete, the fractures in an ideal case would form the boundaries of hexagonal columns, though we usually see just a series of polygonal cracks which are preserved on the bedding planes of many Devonian rocks.

The feature is best seen in the exposure of the Brownstones of the Lower Devonian in the Wilderness Quarry near Mitcheldean. Closer examination of these polygonal sun cracks often reveals trace fossils, trails made by organisms moving over the lake muds of some 400 million years ago. Similar sun cracks can be seen on the mud floor of the same quarry when hot sunshine follows a period of rain. The sketches, Figures 147 and 148, show a specimen with explanatory diagram and it should be noted that, invariably, the grey-green shales have the sun cracks. This may be due to organic material extracting the oxygen from the ferric oxides to create the grey-green ferrous mineral.

FIG 147

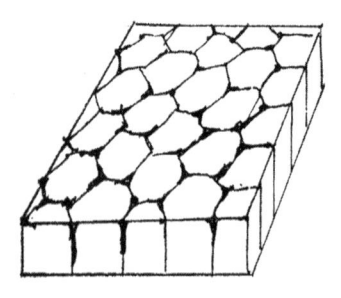

Hexagonal fractures developed from equidistant centres of contraction

FIG 148

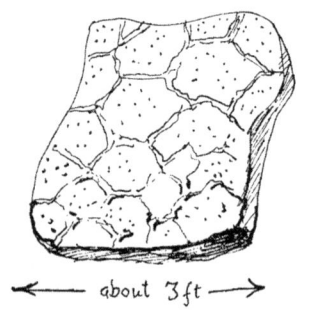

← about 3ft →

Polygonal sun cracks on grey green shale Brownstones

Glossary of terms used in the text

AMMONITES – organisms which had shells usually coiled in a plane (like a snail) but are cephalopods. The Jurassic period was the age of ammonites and they are now extinct.'

ANTHRACONAUTA – a bivalve shell found in the Coal Measures

ANTICLINE – an upfold in strata, like an arch.

BRACHIOPODS – bivalves with a bilateral symmetry.

BRECCIA – a rock containing angular fragments of rock in a matrix.

CHONDRITES – trace fossils – burrowing with infillings in a rock that resemble worm tracks. The kind of organism that left such traces is unknown at present.

CHURN – a term used in the old iron mines indicating a large cavity filled in with iron ore.

CLEAVAGE – the ability of some minerals to split along planes related to the molecular structure of the mineral and parallel to possible crystal faces.

CLINTS – upturned edges of limestone on the surface, a term used in the Pennines where limestone pavements occur naturally and the clint is the rock between vertical fissures called 'grikes'.

CLOD – soft clay or shale lying either above or below a coal seam.

CRINODS – sea lilies, marine animals which grow in colonies on the sea floor.

CYCLOTHEM – layers of sedimentary strata that are often repeated in the same order either above or below the series.

DIASTEM – a special kind of unconformity – a pause in sedimentation. where slight erosion has occurred followed by renewed sedimentation. Usually indicated by rolled fragments of the underlying rock.

DIP – the angle of inclination of strata, measured from the horizontal.

DOLOMITE – a mineral consisting of a double carbonate of magnesium and calcium.

DUNS – Shales overlying the coal seam.

FERRUGINOUS – iron bearing. A ferruginous rock is one in which iron minerals dominate and give it colour.

FOOL'S GOLD – a brassy yellow mineral, iron pyrites, iron sulphide.

GALE – an area of ground below which a miner has mineral rights.

GAVELLER – a Forest of Dean mining official who deals with applicants for gales.

GEODE – a cavity in a rock in which crystals have had room to grow.

GEOMORPHOLOGY – the science that deals with the formation of land forms.

GOETHITE – an iron mineral; an oxide of iron.

GRIKE – small vertical fissure in natural limestone pavement.

HAEMATITE – an oxide of iron.

IGNEOUS ROCKS – rocks which have cooled from the molten state.

KARST TOPOGRAPHY – a special type of limestone scenery caused by solution at the surface and extending downwards.

KEUPER MARL – a red clay kind of rock, forming part of the Triassic system.

LEAT – open water course leading to a mill.

MEANDER – a natural bend on a river.

MONOCLINE – an upfold in strata with only one limb of the fold.

OOLITE – a rock composed of tiny egg – like grains called ooliths.

OROGENY – the process of mountain formation.

OVERSTEP – strata overlying another series that are inclined, so that although some of the lower series may be exposed, the overlying rocks, usually horizontal or nearly so, cover up some of the lower series.

PALAEONTOLOGY – the branch of geology dealing with fossils.

PALAEOZOIC ERA – a period of time in the Earth's history that began about 600 million years ago and lasted about 350 million years. A period in which ancient forms of life occurred.

PALIMPSEST – a manuscript in which the original writing has been effaced to make room for a second, leaving the original faintly visible.

PERICLINE – an upfold in the strata forming a dome – shaped structure, from which strata dip in all directions.

PETROLOGY – a branch of geology dealing with the composition of rocks.

PUDDING STONE – a consolidated gravel conglomerate; the name given by quarry workers to conglomerate

RAFTS – the casts of broken-up tree trunks preserved in sandy rocks often found in Coal Measure sandstones.

RED BEDS – the general name given to strata reddened by ferric oxide and found in continental deposits.

SCOWLES – areas where there are ancient shallow workings for iron ore in Dean.

SIGILLARIA – the name of an extinct tree that lived in Coal Measure times.

SLICKENSIDES – the grooves produced along the plane surfaces of a fault where one mass of rock has slid past another.

STALACTITES – the pinnacles hanging from the roof of a cave or cavity in limestone.

STALAGMITES – the pinnacles found on the floor of a cave or cavity in limestones.

STIGMARIA – the name given to fossil roots of trees found below or above a coal seam.

STREAK PLATE – a plate of unglazed porcelain on which a mineral can be scratched to show its true colour in powder form.

SYNCLINE – a downfold in the strata.

TRAVERTINE – redeposited limestone, often covering the walls of a cave.

TUFA – redeposited limestone from springs in limestone; has plenty of air spaces because the rock consists of both redeposited limestone and moss, grass, twigs, etc.

TRIASSIC PERIOD – a period of geological time that occurred from 200 to 180 million years ago.

UNCONFORMITY – the actual physical break between two series of rocks. It represents a long interval of time between the two different types of sedimentation.

Bibliography

Geology of the Country around Chepstow and Monmouth, Welch and Trotter, HMSO

Geology of the Forest of Dean Coal and Iron Ore Field, Trotter, HMSO

British Regional Geology, Bristol and Gloucester District, Kellaway and Welch, HMSO

Archaeology in Dean, Cyril Hart, John Bellows of Gloucester

Gloucestershire, Finberg, Hodder and Stoughton

Palaeogeography of the Midlands, Wills, University Press of Liverpool

Report of the Forest of Dean Committee, 1958, HMSO

The Face of the Earth, G. H. Dury, Pelican Books

Reports of HM Inspectors of Mines, 1949, South Western Division, HMSO

A Week's Holiday in the Forest of Dean, John Bellows of Gloucester

Nicholls's Forest of Dean, reprint of *The Forest of Dean (1858)* and *Iron-making in the Olden Times* (1866), David & Charles

'The Avon Gorge', R. Bradshaw, Proceedings of the Bristol Naturalists' Society, vol 31, part 2

'Aspects of the Biological Weathering of Limestone Pavement', R. L. Jones, Proceedings of the Geologists' Association, vol 76, part 4

'The Entrenched Meanders of the Herefordshire Wye', Austin Miller, Geography, 1935

'Iron-making in the Forest of Dean', Sibley, paper read before the Iron & Steel Institute (out of print)

Appendix

TABLE OF STRATA SHOWING THE CHIEF ROCK FORMATIONS IN THE DEAN AREA AND WYE VALLEY
(The oldest rocks are at the bottom and the youngest on top)

GEOLOGICAL AGE millions of years	ERA	PERIOD	ROCK FORMATION		AVERAGE THICKNESS IN FEET
225	MESOZOIC	TRIAS		Keuper Marl	300
				Dolomitic Conglomerate	0–50
			...major unconformity...		
280		UPPER CARBONIFEROUS	Upper Coal Measures	*Supra Pennant Group* shales, sandstones and a few coal seams	1,100
				Pennant Group sandstones with shales and a few coal seams	700
				Trenchard Group shales and sandstones with a few coal seams	300
325					
			...major unconformity...		
	PALAEOZOIC	LOWER CARBONIFEROUS	Carboniferous Limestone Series	*Drybrook Sandstone* red to yellow coarse grained sandstone with conglomerates	300
				Whitehead Limestone	100
				Crease Limestone open textured limestone with iron ore pockets	100
				Lower Dolomite pinkish-grey limestone	300
				Lower Limestone Shale crinoidal limestones thinly bedded with shale bands	200
345			...major unconformity...		
		UPPER DEVONIAN		*Tintern Sandstone Group* red to yellow sandstones	300
				Quartz Conglomerate pebbles of quartz in sandstone matrix	100
			...major unconformity...		
		LOWER DEVONIAN		*Brownstones* red brown to grey sandstones	3,000
				St. Maughan's Group red marls and sandstones	1,300
				Raglan Marl Group red marls with sub-ordinate sandstones	1,500
395			...major unconformity...		
		SILURIAN			

N.B. *In Dean, the Middle Carboniferous, Millstone Grit Division and Lower Coal Measures are not represented.*

Index

Agrostis tenuis 142
Alethopteris 152
Annularia 152
Anthraconauta 155
Ariconium 133
Astonbridge Hill 33, 157
Astridge Barn 100
Aust 24
Avonmouth Docks 119
Awre 167
Aylburton 53
Bailey Gate 61
Bailey Level 66
Bailey Point 60, 63, 65
Ban-y-gor Rocks 111
Ban-y-gor rocks 115, 117, 118
Barnedge Hill 33
Barnhill Plantation 139, 144
Beachley 24, 58
Beachley-Clanna pericline 50, 52
Bearse Farm 165
Beechenhurst 149
Berkeley Canal 49
Berkeley canal 57
Biblins 76, 79, 86
Bigsweir 102, 104, 105, 108, 123, 165
Bill Mill 63
Bircham Wood 158, 161
Bishopswood 158
Bixhead 144, 153
Bixslade stone works 139
Blackpool Bridge 43, 44, 45, 46
Blackpool Brook 43
Blackrock Farm 52
Black Cliff 111
Blakeney 36, 43, 44, 50
Brachiopods 83
Brachypodia 88
Breakheart Hill 27
Bream 64, 129
Bream Tufts 129
Brierley 33, 142
British Mine 131
Brockweir 109
Brooks Head Grove 165
Brownstones 27, 36, 44, 46, 48, 51, 54, 59, 62, 72, 98, 105, 106, 161, 168
Buckshraft 42, 133
Buckstone 99, 108, 123
Bunter Sandstone 56
Caerwent syncline 115
Calamites 57, 152
Calcite 81
Calcium 113
Cannop 135, 139, 143, 146, 149
Cannop Brook 51
Cannop Ponds 141
Chapel Hill 110
Chase House 115
Chase Wood 66, 72, 73
Cheltenham 12
Chepstow 14, 16, 17, 25, 68, 98, 111, 113, 115, 117, 118, 120, 122
Chestnuts Inclosure 37
Chondrites 41, 83
Cinderfor 38
Cinderford 41, 42, 133, 135, 141
Clanna 24
Clanna pericline 59
Clanna Woods 53

Clearwell 107, 129, 130, 158, 161
Clearwell Meend 131
Cleddon Shoots 108
Cleeve Hill 9
Clements Tump 130
Cliff Farm 55
Clints 163
Coalification 153
Cobrey Park 73
Coldwell Rocks 79, 91
Coleford 101, 115, 124, 131
Coleford High Delf 35, 91, 141, 144, 148
Composite 119
Cone 54
Cone Brook 53
Coppet Hill 75, 82, 84
Cotswolds 19
Crease Limestone 39, 41, 64, 82, 85, 89, 91, 114, 120, 124, 129, 135, 137, 139
Crease Limestone. 122
Crinoidal limestone 165
Crinoids 83
Cyclothem 155
Danby Lodge 19, 45, 46, 47, 49
Dancing Green 62
Deanpool 131
Deanpool Farm 130
Delves 133
Dennel Hill 117
Devil's Chapel 124, 125, 127, 130
Devil's Ditch 127
Devil's Pulpit 111, 113
Devil's Chapel 64
Devonian Conglomerate 47
Dolomite 80, 81, 115
Dolomitic Conglomerate 17, 55, 58

Dropping Wells 86
Drummer Boy Stone 47, 135
Drybrook 61
Drybrook Limestone 16, 118, 120
Drybrook Sandstone 14, 16, 31, 40, 42, 60, 64, 65, 89, 115, 116, 117, 119, 133, 135, 137
Eastern United Colliery 149
Edgehills 39, 133
Edge End 144
Edge Hills 30
English Bicknor 76
Equisetum 57
Euroclydon 61
Evesham 12
Festuca rubra 142
Flaxley 135
Fool's gold 153
Forest of Dean Caving Society 131
Foy 74
Free mining 151
Frogmore 73
Gabion basket 96
Garwoodia 65
Garwoodia gregaria 113
Gatcombe 49
Geochronometry 10
Geodes 81
Goethite 140
Goodrich Castle 72
Greathough Brook valley 157
Greathough valley 33
Great Doward 84, 88, 89
Green Bottom 41
Grikes 163
Grove Wood 121
Hadnock Quarry 83, 92
Haematite 81, 126, 131, 140
Hangerberry 132

Index

Hardwick Quarry 122
Hardwick quarry 113, 114
Harold Stones 107
Harry Hill 32
Hayes Coppice 92, 93
Hereford 74, 75
Hewelsfield 54, 105, 109
Highbury Plain 100, 105
High Beech 35
Hock Cliff 167
Holcus lanatus 142
Hope Mansel 59, 60, 62, 63
Horse Lea Hill 34
Howle Hill 59
Huntsham bridge 76
Huntsham Hill 82, 83, 84
Huntsham hill 83
Ichthyosaurus 166
Iron making 124
Jacob's Ladder 55
Jasper 84
Joy's Green 34
Joyford Mill 165
Kerne Bridge 67, 69, 72, 75
Keuper Marl 17, 24, 36, 56, 58, 138
Kings Caple 74
King Arthur's Cave 90, 132
King Arthur's cave 89
Knackers Hole Grove 63
Kymin 97
Lambsquay Wood 131
Lancaut 77, 111, 123
Lea 36
Lea Bailey 62
Lepidodendron 152
Lindors Farm 103
Lithification 113
Lithostrotion martini 119

Littledean 36, 37, 133
Little Doward 83, 90, 92
Liveoaks 111, 113, 115, 117, 118, 123
Livox Quarry 113
Livox Wood 98
Llandogo 108
Lodges Barn 100
Longstone 79
Lords Wood 90
Lower Dolomite 54, 81, 82, 86, 99, 111, 113, 115, 117, 122, 128, 130, 137, 144, 163
Lower Limestone Shale 158
Lower Lydbrook 34, 166
Lydbrook 121, 132, 157
Lydney 19, 43, 46, 49, 50, 51
Lydney Park 52, 128
Mailscot Wood 84
Malvern axis 64
Malvern Line 12, 21, 22, 25, 27
Mansel dome 66
May Hill 27, 64
May Hill-Malvern Axis 38
Meanders 69
Meering Pond 31
Merlin's Cave 89, 132
Minepit Wood 110, 138
Mitcheldean 28, 37, 65, 72, 115, 133, 168
Mitcheldeania 65
Monmouth 75, 89, 92, 111
Moseley Green 46
Nailbridge 31, 32, 161
Near Hearkening Rock 84
Neuropteris 152
Newland 99, 100, 101, 102, 103, 124, 158, 161
Newnham 38, 43

New Mills 51
Nofold Green 150
Norchard Colliery 51
Norchard Wood 51
Northern United Colliery 32, 149, 161
Noxon Park 129
Offa's Dyke 56, 91
Offa's dyke 10
Offa's Dyke 111
Oldbury 57
Old Ham Mine 131, 140
Old Park Wood 127
Oolith 87
open-cast mining 150
Ostrea liassica 56
Palmer's Flat 62
Parkend 43, 135, 146
Parkend High Delf 149
Parsons Allotment 165
Penalt 98, 107
Pennant sandstone 16, 34, 35, 139, 141, 143, 144, 146
Pennant sandstones 153
Penyard Park 66, 72
Piercefield Cliffs 113, 119
Piercfield 111
Pluds 98, 99
Plump Hill 29, 31, 34, 36, 41, 133, 141
Point Inn 29, 30, 32
Polygonal cracks 168
Pontshill 59
Poor's Allotment 115, 116
Pope's Hill 36
Primrose Hill 51, 52
Princess Royal Colliery 149
Priors Mesne 50, 53
Productus 119

Pteridosperms 152
Pudding stone 15
Puddlebrook 41, 59, 60, 63
Purton 43
Quartz Conglomerat 97
Quartz Conglomerate 38, 41, 50, 52, 53, 59, 61, 63, 66, 70, 75, 82, 84, 91, 92, 98, 99, 104, 105, 107, 108, 122, 135, 161
Queen Stone 91
The Rudge 62
Redbrook 100, 105, 108
Red beds 136
Rock Inn 91
Rodmore 53
Romans 52
Rosemary Topping 79
Ross 67, 68, 69, 73, 74
Ross church 67, 72
Rowley 54
Ruardean Hill 23, 123, 144, 147, 157
Ruspidge 42, 133, 141, 161
Scowles 41, 52, 64, 110, 124, 131
Scully Grove 65, 115
Sedbury Cliff 56, 58
Sedimentation 155
Seven Sisters 111
Seven Sisters Rocks 86
Severn 38, 56, 73
Severn bridge 24, 53, 58
Severn estuary 53, 98
Severn Vale 36
Shakemantle 133, 161
Shakemantle Quarry 42
Sharpness 49
Sigillaria 145, 152
Sinkholes 165
Slickensides 163

Index

Smith, William 9
Soudley 36, 44, 47, 48, 133, 135
Soudley Brook 43
Spartina townsendi 57
Speech House 141
Staple Edge 148
Staple Edge Wood 42
Staunton 84, 99, 132
Staunton Meend 99
Steam Mills 150
Stigmaria 143, 149
Stow 163
Stowe 105
St Annal's iron-mine 39
St Anthony's Well 42
St Briavels 101, 103, 116, 161, 165, 166
St Maughan's group 48, 49, 54, 55, 96, 97
Suckstone 84, 108
Sun cracks 168
Supra Pennant 141, 150
Swallets 165
Swallow holes 165
Symond's Yat 10, 16, 29, 43, 69, 75, 76, 106
Ten-Acre Wood 149
Ten Acre Wood 52
Thomas Wood 75
Tidenham 24, 50, 53, 54, 117, 138, 158
Tidenham Chase 116, 123, 165
Tintem Abbey 98, 110
Tintem Quarry 67, 116
Tintem Sandstone 110
Tintem Sandstones 30
Tintern 117
Tintern Abbey 105, 108, 109, 111
Tintern Quarry 115, 117
Tintern Sandstone 15, 61, 83, 99, 107, 165
Travertine 86, 163
Trelleck 107, 108, 123
Trenchard series 52, 64, 91, 143, 144, 149
Tudorville 67, 73
Tufa 57
Two Bridges 48
Upper Lydbrook 31, 34, 41
Viney Hill 43, 44
Sir John Wintour iron works 128
Walford 72, 73
Westbury Brook Mine 133
Weston-under-Penyard 61, 73
West Tump Inn 44
Whitchurch 76
Whitecliff 131
Whitecroft 149
Whitehead Limestone 65, 113, 115, 117
Wigpool 14, 59, 60, 64, 65
Wigpool Mine 64, 66, 133
Wigpool syncline 60, 63, 66
Wilderness Quarry 27, 30, 72, 168
Willscroft Wood 165
Wimberry Slade 142, 149
Wintour's Leap 111, 118, 119
Woodcroft 118
Woolaston 50, 54
Worcester Lodge 139
Wyastone Leys 91, 92
Wye meander 74
Wynd Cliff 118, 138, 165
Yankee Cinema 64
Yat Rock 76, 79, 80, 82, 83, 91, 132

www.fineleaf.co.uk